MOTIVATING YOUR SALES F<

By the same author

Beyond the Pay-Packet
Face the Press
How to Recruit and Select Successful Salesmen (2nd edition)
Making Effective Presentations (audio manual)
Manual of Sales Negotiation
Marketing Planning for the Pharmaceutical Industry
Motivating your Sales Force
Negotiating Profitable Sales
The Sales Presentation (jointly)
Training Salesmen on the Job (2nd edition)

Motivating Your Sales Force

JOHN LIDSTONE

Gower

Published by
Gower Publishing Limited
Gower House
Croft Road
Aldershot
Hampshire GU11 3HR
England

Gower
Old Post Road
Brookfield
Vermont 05036
USA

British Library Cataloguing-in-Publication Data. A catalogue record for this
book is available from the British Library.

ISBN 0 566 07617 9

Printed in Great Britain at the University Press, Cambridge

Contents

List of tables

List of figures

Preface

Motivating a Sales Force is one of the most important and continuous tasks of every Sales Manager. It is also one of the most difficult. First, because unlike a new car for example which comes with the manufacturer's manual telling you how to drive and maintain it, salesmen and saleswomen are not quite so accommodating. Everyone is different with his or her own unique pattern of needs, drives and hungers; far more complicated than any machine. But when we appoint them or become responsible for them people do not hand us a personal instruction manual telling us *how* to motivate them.

Secondly, despite the vast amount of legislation governing such aspects as the protection of employment and equal opportunities for women, few companies equip managers before they are appointed - or afterwards - with a sufficient body of knowledge about what influences human behaviour and motivation to enable them to bring an informed approach to managing people. Consequently for most sales managers their biggest problem is that the whole subject of motivation is characterised by a lack of knowledge of the human needs and motives of their salesmen and of expertise in *how* to motivate them.

It is therefore hardly surprising that the motivational policies far too many managers bring to managing sales forces are coloured by their personal standards and hunches, prejudices and assumptions - rarely substantiated by facts.

The environment in which sales managers seek to achieve planned sales objectives *through* their sales forces - *and not for them* - is a very different one from that of even ten years ago. Today sales managers are managing *salesmen* and *saleswomen*. For many this is a new and awesome experience. Companies are getting larger in size yet fewer in number. In many markets this involves fewer but far more highly trained and skilled salesmen — difficult to find and costly to lose and replace. Unlike the past when salesmen could be fired at will, it is increasingly difficult to get rid of people.

For all these reasons managers must become more knowledgeable and skilled in retaining and motivating their sales forces to achieve results in a tougher and more competitive commercial environment. Hence this book. Its purpose is twofold. First, to offer a framework of understanding about human behaviour and the factors that influence it; and secondly, to provide practical guidelines which can be used to develop a realistic programme designed to motivate your sales force.

Who should use it?

First, it is written for the sales manager with day-to-day responsibility for managing and motivating a sales force. He or she may be called country manager, regional, area or district sales manager; may be working in Brussels or Brisbane, Scunthorpe or Singapore; may be managing an industrial, service, capital goods or fast moving consumer goods sales force.

It is written for a second and equally important group; for managing directors, marketing directors and sales directors. Why? Because if I were to summarise the bitter experiences voiced by thousands of middle and first line sales managers throughout the world with whom I have discussed motivation and to whom I have proposed solutions to their problems it would be on these lines: 'We agree with you. You are preaching to the converted. But you should be telling this to our directors. They send us to you to be developed and then ignore our recommendations.'

The book will also, I hope, prove useful reading for personnel and training managers.

Content

In the first chapter I have described in simple terms the theories of four people whose analyses of human behaviour have, in my judgement, had the most influence upon managerial thinking and approaches to motivating people at work and in particular sales forces. Unlike mathematics, the study of human behaviour is not an exact science. My aim has been to give managers no one theory but a background against which they can hammer out a policy that 'works for me'.

The second chapter seeks to define leadership in the context of the real world in which selling takes place. Wherever managers meet today to discuss the needs of workers the cry goes up that 'everyone wants to participate'. I think that a great deal of this talk is spurious. Yes, people do want to be consulted about and participate in the things that concern them, but they also want the smack of firm government in their work and no group needs this more than salesmen.

Chapters 3-7 examine the motivations which have been identified as most important to salesmen in every industry and all over the world, and set out practical ways these needs can be met.

In Chapter 8 I have put forward two techniques by which sales managers can identify the needs of their salesmen and saleswomen so that a more informed approach can be brought to the motivation of the sales force and to those individuals who comprise it. Chapter 9 is designed to help you develop a practical programme for action in relation to your own sales force.

Finally, in Chapter 10 I describe the job of the sales manager: to achieve his/her overall task objective of getting planned sales objectives through the efforts of the sales force must, above all, know how to motivate them to do so.

John Lidstone
May 1994

1 Theories of motivation

Of all the skills required by sales managers, the one that is perhaps most widely misunderstood and so practised with the least effectiveness is motivation.

Whenever one hears managers discuss this subject their views, approaches and solutions are constant reminders that much management practice in this vital area is surrounded by folklore. The following are, in summary, examples of some approaches:

'He was an army officer, so he knows how to handle men.'

'All they are interested in is money.'

'I don't want to see my salesmen, they should be out selling.'

'I use planned insecurity. I fire the man at the bottom of the sales league each month. It works like a dream.'

'They have a job here for life - what more do they want?'

The main stumbling block standing between sales managers and their ability to achieve sustained and satisfactory sales results through their sales force is probably their lack of knowledge and expertise in the whole subject of motivation and human behaviour. This ignorance of what really makes a salesman or saleswoman tick leads to the formulation of so-called motivational policies and plans which do not correspond to the repertoire of the individual needs of the majority of salesmen in a sales force. This results in sales forces operating at sixty per cent or less in effectiveness, in commitment to the job to be performed and in the quality and quantity of sales achieved.

1.1 What do we mean by motivation?

To develop our understanding of this complex, fascinating and vital subject we first need to be quite clear what we mean by motivation. The word motive from which it comes means: 'That which moves or induces a person to act in a certain way; that which tends to move a person to a course of action.' So to motivate is: 'to cause someone to act in a particular way; to furnish with a motive'.

Motivation then is concerned on the one hand with understanding each individual salesman's and saleswoman's internal needs and emotions and then providing inducements which will result in men and women wanting to employ their full abilities in their work.

1

Dostoyevsky wrote: 'Man never acts from a single motive.' Every individual has within him certain needs, drives and hungers and it is these inner forces which spur him into action. As a generalisation we all have a need for money; to feel secure; for status; for job satisfaction; for power; to compete and so on. The extent to which we need these motivating elements will differ markedly. It is in the differences that we define, recognise and attempt to satisfy, that lies success in motivating salesmen.

Many of these needs are satisfied independently of the job. But there are others - we can call them *job motivations* - which can be and often must be satisfied by or on the job that a person does. The satisfaction of these job motivations provides the reasons why people work; why they choose one job rather than another; why they stick to one job and above all why they like their jobs.

Your task as a sales manager is to achieve your planned profit and sales targets through the combined efforts of all your salesmen *who want to reach the same objectives.* And therein lies the challenge and the question: if each one reaches his individual planned sales target will he also satisfy his personal needs as well as yours? And how will you know anyway?

You can only harness the efforts of your salesmen and move them to act to produce the results you want if you have identified the factors that are prominent in influencing human behaviour.

Theories about what influences mankind are legion. Many psychologists, behavioural scientists and work study experts have added to our knowledge of human behaviour and have influenced successive strategies companies have used to motivate their staffs to achieve the organisation's objectives and goals. We will examine the theories of four people who have had a major influence upon the approaches to motivating people adopted by commercial organisations in the last half century. These theorists are: F. W. Taylor, A. Maslow, Douglas McGregor, and Frederick Herzberg.

1.2 F. W. Taylor: scientific management

Towards the end of the nineteenth century world trade was increasing, and industrial competition with it. The need began to be felt for a more scientific approach to management. Work study was applied with the aim of producing a system in which workers' time would be utilised to achieve maximum production and wasted time would be minimised.

The 'scientific management' methods of F. W. Taylor which were developed in industry in the early years of this century were based on the Law of Effect or the principle of reinforcement. This states: If a person undertakes an action and this action is followed by a reward - the probability that the action will be repeated is increased. Conversely, if a person undertakes an action which is either ignored or followed by a punishment, this behaviour is less likely to be repeated.

Taylor claimed that through a policy of effective staff selection, training based upon specific defined standards, monitoring of performance, and allocation of rewards and punishments based on observed performance, people will perform to required expectations. The limitations of this approach are that

1   It satisfies basic needs but not the higher ones.
2   It relies on objective methods of assessing performance.
3   It is ineffective where individual effort cannot be precisely identified.
4   It is ineffective where, although the job is being performed to all the standards set, adverse market conditions inhibit sales success.
5   Disputes will arise where rewards and punishments are not under the control of the individual.

Although many companies incorporate elements of Taylor's scientific management in their policies today, it should be remembered that it evolved and took root in a very different economic and social environment. Unemployment was very high, and there were few if any social security benefits such as are common in many countries today.

1.3   Maslow's hierarchy of needs

In the wake of the famous Hawthorne experiments of 1924-32 a wave of research swept through industry concerned with the social implications of work. Notable among the earliest workers in this field was Abraham Maslow, whose thinking was to have a profound influence in the following two decades. Maslow suggested that man is a 'perpetually wanting animal' whose needs are organised in a series of levels - a hierarchy of importance (see Figure 1.1).

Physiological needs
At the lowest level are man's physiological needs based upon his need to survive, e.g. for food, for water, air, rest, exercise, warmth, shelter from the elements. Man lives by bread alone when there is little bread. His

3

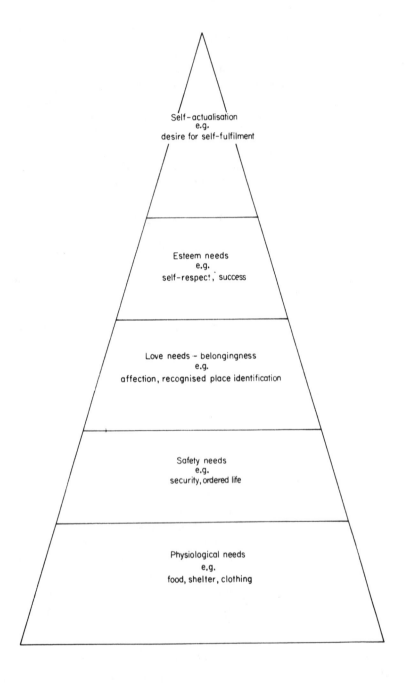

Self-actualisation
e.g.
desire for self-fulfilment

Esteem needs
e.g.
self-respect, success

Love needs - belongingness
e.g.
affection, recognised place identification

Safety needs
e.g.
security, ordered life

Physiological needs
e.g.
food, shelter, clothing

Fig. 1.1   Maslow's hierarchy of needs

needs for love and for status do not loom large in importance when his belly has been empty for a long time. Only when man's physiological needs are satisfied on a regular and continuing basis do they cease to be important. If you saw the film *King Rat* about prisoners of war starving in the Far East you will remember that, just to survive, men with cultivated tastes in food and other things in life were ready to trade anything they could lay their hands on - jewellery, gold teeth fillings - for the cooked rat meat which one entrepreneurial prisoner was selling secretly in the prison compound.

Safety needs

Once these basic needs are satisfied on a regular basis, higher needs arise and these rather than the physiological needs now dominate man's attention and motivation. This new level of needs relates to safety. The average person needs and prefers to have a safe, organised, orderly, predictable life and to reduce to the minimum the unpredictable or exposure to danger. In a well organised peaceful society individuals rarely have any safety needs as an active motivator. In this sense, just as a man with a full belly is no longer hungry, a safe man no longer feels endangered.

Love needs

If both the physiological and the safety needs are satisfied, then man's need for love, for affection and to belong will emerge to be satisfied and the whole cycle will repeat itself with these new needs. Now a person will feel keenly the absence of friends, a sweetheart or a wife and children. In the larger community he will seek to have friendly relationships and a recognised place. Similarly he will strive after the same relationships in the work group. The intensity with which individuals will seek the goal of such relationships can be measured by the ruthlessness with which work groups can send one of their number 'to Coventry' for failing to conform to group (or union) decisions.

Maslow distinguished love at this level of need from sex. Sex can be studied as a physiological need in the context of mankind's need to perpetuate his own species. This is not to say that sexual behaviour is not aroused by other needs such as love and affection and even status.

Dr Robert McMurry in his paper 'The Mystique of Super Salesmanship'[1] attributes the mystique of super salesmanship to individuals who have a compulsive need to win and hold the affection of others. These commercial wooers are not born with this need. It is the product of early environment characterised by the absence of love and affection, the conviction that they really are unloved and unwanted. Their reac-

5

tion is to use every means at their disposal in an attempt to win or 'buy' the affection of those with whom they come into contact: charm, flattery, presents and similar inducements. Such people are very sensitive to every move and inflection and have a great empathy towards others. These are the salesmen so often described as those who 'never stop selling'.

Esteem needs

Most people in society have a need for a stable, firmly based high evaluation of themselves, for self-esteem and for the respect and esteem of others. Satisfaction of this need for self-esteem on a continuing basis leads to feelings of self-confidence, worth, strength and conviction of one's own capabilities and above all of being useful and necessary in the world.

The need for self-actualisation (for self-fulfilment)

Even when all these four levels of needs are satisfied, we may still often, as 'perpetually wanting animals', experience a new discontent and restlessness unless we are doing what we believe we are fitted for. Even though a man is turning a lathe in a factory, if he believes he can and must paint, or make music, he will only ultimately be happy if he fulfils himself by learning to paint or to play an instrument either as an absorbing hobby or, in the long term, as a full-time activity. This crowning need Maslow called self-actualisation or the desire for self-fulfilment.

Maslow originally presented his theory as a tentative basis for organising motives. He confessed himself 'a little worried about this stuff, which I consider to be tentative, being swallowed whole by all sorts of enthusiastic people'.

On this cautionary note we can nevertheless consider our own experiences in managing and motivating salesmen. Certainly the interwoven nature of individual needs suggests that the normal adult human being cannot go to work with say two preponderant levels of need, having left the other three at home. All five accompany him to work. But in acknowledging this fact it should be remembered that some are possibly being satisfied independently of the job he does. *A satisfied need is not a motivator of human behaviour.*

1.4 McGregor's Theory *X* and Theory *Y*

One of the management thinkers strongly influenced by Maslow was Douglas McGregor. In *The Human Side of Enterprise*, first published

6

in 1960, McGregor wrote: 'behind every managerial decision or action are assumptions about human nature and human behaviour.' He labelled two widely held assumptions Theory X and Theory Y (see Table 1.1).

Theory X assumes that:

1 Man is a wanting animal who has an inherent dislike of work itself and will avoid it if he can.
2 He therefore requires continuing coercion, control and threats to keep him at work and performing adequately.
3 The average man prefers being directed, has a craving for security and is unwilling to assume responsibility.

From the advocates of Theory X stems a pattern of management in which the motivation of staff is confined to the manipulation of rewards and punishments.

1 Management is responsible for organising the elements of productive enterprise - money, material, equipment, people - in the interests of economic ends.
2 With respect to people, this is a process of directing their efforts, motivating them, controlling their actions, modifying their behaviour to fit the needs of the organisation.
3 Without this assertive intervention by management, people would be passive - even resistant - to organisational needs.

Theory X shares with Taylor's scientific management the carrot and stick approach to motivation and it can be argued that this works effectively in certain conditions, e.g. when an individual is glad of a job and wages to satisfy the most basic needs of life - providing the means to subsist. In an age of comparative affluence, Theory X fails to motivate. For this reason McGregor proposed a contrasting and much more optimistic theory for managing and motivating people which he called Theory Y:

1 Putting effort into work is as natural as rest or play. The average human being does not dislike work but, depending on conditions, work is a source of satisfaction to be voluntarily performed, not a source of punishment to be avoided.
2 Man will exercise self-direction and self-control to achieve objectives to which he is personally committed.
3 Commitment to objectives is a function of rewards associated with achieving those objectives.
4 Under proper conditions, the average person learns not only to accept but to seek responsibility.
5 The capacity to exercise imagination, ingenuity and creativity is

7

Table 1.1

Theory *X* and Theory *Y*

Behind every managerial decision or action are assumptions about human nature and behaviour. In his book The Human Side of Enterprise *Douglas McGregor crystallised two fundamental viewpoints which he called* **Theory X** *and* **Theory Y**. *These have entered management folklore in the last decade, but there are few who could quote them.*

Theory X states a traditional management view of direction and control. It offers management an easy rationalisation for ineffective organisational performance - it is due to the nature of the human resources with which they must work.

Theory Y draws together knowledge of man from many new sources and states that the limits of human collaboration in the organisational setting are not limits of human nature, but of management skill in discovering how to realise abundant but latent human potentiality and resources.

Theory *X*

1 *The average human being has an inherent dislike of work and will avoid it if he can.*

This assumption has deep roots ... The stress that management places on productivity, on the concept of 'a fair day's work', on the evils of featherbedding and restriction of output, on rewards for performance - while it has a logic in terms of the objectives of enterprise - reflects an underlying belief that management must counteract an inherent human tendency to avoid work...

2 *Because of this human characteristic of dislike of work, most people must be coerced, controlled, directed, threatened with punishment to get them to put forth adequate effort towards the*

Theory *Y*

1 *The expenditure of physical and mental effort in work is as natural as play or rest.* The average human being does not inherently dislike work. Depending upon controllable conditions, work may be a source of satisfaction (and will be voluntarily performed) or a source of punishment (and will be avoided if possible).

2 *External control and the threat of punishment are not the only means for bringing about effort towards organisational objectives. Man will exercise self-direction and self-control in the service of objectives to which he is committed.*

3 *Commitment to objectives is a function of the rewards asso-*

achievement of organisational objectives.

The dislike of work is so strong that even the promise or rewards is not generally enough to overcome it. People will accept the rewards and demand continually higher ones, but these alone will not produce the necessary effort. Only the threat of punishment will do the trick . . . .

3 *The average human being prefers to be directed, wishes to avoid responsibility, has relatively little ambition, wants security above all.*

This assumption of the 'mediocrity of the masses' is rarely expressed so bluntly. In fact a good deal of lip service is given to the ideal of the worth of the average human being. Our political and social values demand such public expressions. Nevertheless, a great many managers will give private support to this assumption, and it is easy to see it reflected in policy and practice. Paternalism has become a nasty word, but it is by no means a defunct managerial philosophy.

ciated with their achievement. The most significant of such rewards, e.g. the satisfaction of ego and self-actualisation needs, can be direct products of effort directed towards organisational objectives.

4 *The average human being learns, under proper conditions, not only to accept but to seek responsibility.* Avoidance of responsibility, lack of ambition, and emphasis on security, are generally consequences of experience, not inherent human characteristics.

5 *The capacity to exercise a relatively high degree of imagination, ingenuity, and creativity in the solution of organisational problems is widely, not narrowly, distributed in the population.*

6 *Under the conditions of modern industrial life, the intellectual potentialities of the average human being are only partially utilised.*

---

      widely distributed throughout the population.
  6 Under the conditions of modern commercial and industrial life the potential of the average human being is underutilised.

Assuming that Theory *Y* mirrors reality more than Theory *X* McGregor suggests that:

  1 Management is responsible for organising the elements of productive enterprise - money, materials, equipment, people - in the interests of economic ends.

2 People are *not* by nature passive or resistant to organisational needs. They have become so as a result of experience in organisations.

3 The motivation, the potential for development, the capacity for assuming responsibility, the readiness to direct behaviour towards organisational goals, are all present in people. Management does not put them there. But management has the responsibility to make it possible for people to recognise and develop these human characteristics for themselves.

4 The essential task of management is to arrange organisational conditions and methods of operation so that people can achieve their own goals *best* by directing *their own* efforts towards organisational objectives.

Theory *X* and Theory *Y* are poles apart in their assumptions. Theory *X* places almost exclusive reliance on external controls of human behaviour whilst Theory *Y* relies heavily on self-control and self-direction. The differences are as between treating people as children and treating them as mature adults. McGregor recognised that after generations had been treated as children in the work environment we cannot expect to shift to treating them as adults overnight. The application of theory is always a slow process.

In practice, as you will recognise, a path has to be taken between these two extremes of Theory *X* and Theory *Y* in evolving an effective approach to motivating and controlling a sales force. We will return to this subject particularly in the context of styles of leadership later.

1.5 Herzberg's satisfiers and dissatisfiers

Since the publication of his book *Work and the Nature of Man*, in 1968, a great deal of research into motivation has been stimulated by Professor Frederick Herzberg. In respect of sales management in particular he has contributed in a practical way to a better understanding of the factors that influence and motivate sales personnel.

Drawing on the studies and findings of many professional colleagues including Maslow, his researches attempted to identify and analyse the factors that give rise to satisfying and dissatisfying experiences at work. Analysing thousands of responses from groups of workers performing identical jobs from hospital workers and salesmen to credit control correspondence clerks produced a remarkably consistent and surprising result.

Two separate sets of factors are found to be at the root of satisfaction and dissatisfaction.

Dissatisfiers

Those factors which tended to cause dissatisfaction were generally found to be connected with the environment in which people worked. These 'hygiene factors', as Herzberg called them because they need cleaning up regularly, tend more often than not to produce dissatisfaction than satisfaction. The most common and frequently mentioned factors causing dissatisfaction were: company policy and administration; supervision; interpersonal relationships with one's superiors; with one's equals; with one's subordinates; working conditions; personal life; status; security and salary. Looking at this list you might be tempted to say, 'well if a person's salary is unsatisfactory and I put it right then surely the individual will be motivated.' Herzberg's research suggested that the removal of a source of dissatisfaction does not necessarily result in positive motivation. Rather, if all the sources of dissatisfaction are removed an individual is not made happy but ceases to be unhappy. He is in a 'neutral' position (see Figure 1.2).

Another finding about dissatisfiers was that the effect of putting them right tends to be short-lived. Thus time and taxes can soon erode a

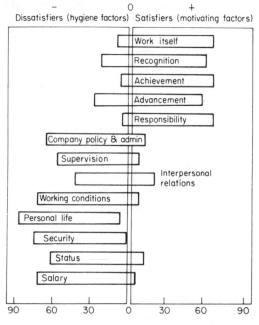

Fig. 1.2   Herzberg's satisfiers and dissatisfiers

salary increase. If salaries are reviewed annually, for example - as they are in most companies - an increase will lose its psychological impact long before the next one becomes due.

In short, neither removing causes of dissatisfaction nor 'cleaning up' the environment in which the job is performed will motivate effectively.

Satisfiers

The other set of factors which contributed to experiencing job satisfaction and motivation centred on the job itself and the intrinsic possibilities it provided to meet an individual's highest personal goals and needs for self-fulfilment. These factors, capable of producing positive and more enduring motivation, were found to be: work itself; recognition; opportunities for advancement; responsibility; achievement; possibilities of personal growth.

Positive steps taken by management to enrich these areas of potential satisfaction are longer lasting in their effect and impact upon individuals than the removal of sources of dissatisfaction. If you give a man a fish you feed him for a day, but it will not stop him feeling hungry tomorrow, whereas if you teach him how to fish he acquires the skill to feed himself for life.

If the theories of Maslow and Herzberg are put together the dissatisfiers or hygiene factors are the commercial and industrial expression of the first three levels in the hierarchy - the physiological, safety and love needs. The motivators or satisfiers correspond to the upper hierarchical needs for esteem and self-fulfilment.

Herzberg verified his theories in a number of commercial and industrial organisations in Europe and the UK as well as in the USA. Its importance is not only the extent to which it complements and extends the researches and theories about man at work of other psychologists but the insight it provides into how levels of human need operate at work. The traditional approach and solutions - increasing financial incentives, better working conditions and greater job security - are important in keeping employees from being dissatisfied but this is all they are likely to achieve. The commitment and extra effort from people will come from considering what they do as well as how they are treated.

1.6 Conclusion

There is a danger when considering the four theories that have been quoted in this chapter and others which are attracting itinerant followers such as Management by Objectives, to assume that everyone is hell bent on the search for developing their potential and achieving self-fulfilment.

Certainly Dr Robert McMurry with whom I have worked on a number of assignments and who has studied many thousands of employees, particularly in sales, refutes this argument. So does David McClelland, Professor of Psychology at Harvard University. Both lean towards the conclusion that there is a minority - perhaps ten at most fifteen per-cent - which is motivated and challenged by opportunity and willing to work hard to achieve something. But the majority are not.

The marketing environment in which selling takes place creates other factors which influence salesman behaviour and motivation which we shall examine in Chapter 2. What are the most important job motivations of salesmen which influence their selling performance? During the last eight years, 1,860 sales and field sales managers from every type of commercial, industrial and service company operating in the UK, the nine countries in the European Economic Community, in South East Asia, Nigeria, in Australia and New Zealand have been asked this question. They all wrote down the following five motivational influences which are not listed in any order or priority. Questionnaires completed by their salesmen produced an identical list: remuneration; direct incentives; security; status; and job satisfaction. If the first two are coupled together and we assume that a major proportion of what a salesman is paid is spent on buying the necessities of life - a house, food, clothing etc. - then three in this list are to be found among the causes of potential dissatisfaction. This is a timely reminder of how carefully sales management needs to forecast and deal with problems in these areas before they arise. Sadly all too often managers spend their time fighting problems which could have been foreseen, as examples later in the book will illustrate.

Under the heading of job satisfaction many responses qualified their answer with additions such as: recognition, advancement, ambition, desire to compete/achieve, and to excel. Interestingly these approximate to many of Herzberg's motivators and to the upper levels of Maslow's hierarchy of needs.

Because motivation is too vital a subject to be left to chance, sales managers cannot evade their responsibilities for their salesmen. To get the best results through your salesmen involves knowing what motivates each individual member of your team and then bringing different approaches to each one which reflect their individual pattern of needs and motivations. In the following chapters we shall explore the five major motivational influences that have been identified and show how you can develop a repertoire of techniques to enable you to satisfy the needs of your salesmen, and through doing so achieve your managerial objectives.

Note

[1] Robert McMurry, 'The Mystique of Super Salesmanship,' *Harvard Business Review*, March/April 1961.

2 The selling job

Selling - the art and skill of persuading people to buy products, services or ideas - is not a unitary activity. Selling jobs can and do differ in complexity, in interests, in rewards and not least in the kinds of people each type of job attracts. At one end of the spectrum are the relatively simple jobs such as that of a sales assistant serving customers behind a counter in a shop, departmental store or showroom. At the other are such complex and demanding ones as those involving perhaps negotiating the sales of heavy industrial machinery to large industrial organisations or to government departments.

Many sales managers believe that if a person can sell effectively say grocery products, he will not only be equally successful selling industrial products or intangibles such as insurance but could be motivated to do so. Whilst every sales manager can quote success stories to prove his point, there are dangers in taking this assumption (or wishful thinking) too far. Selling is far from being a progressive vocation in which people start at a certain basic level and *automatically* can and do graduate through stages to different and more complex types of sales activity.

The motivational implications of these differing types of selling activity are considerable and sales managers must be aware of them. Paradoxically many of the most difficult sales jobs are the easiest to obtain, for example selling speciality products such as double glazing, encyclopaedias, household hardware, or life assurance largely because they are paid on a commission only basis. Such jobs have also been the graveyard of thousands of sales careers. In many such markets companies assume that the prospect of high commission earnings will act as a self-motivating carrot to salesmen and women. This is generally not true as we shall see later in this chapter.

Nine distinct types of sales position can be identified (as shown in Table 2.1). Most sales jobs are combinations of one or more of these categories, for example a service and sales engineer or a bank manager. A closer examination of these nine categories, however, reveals some important distinctions which must be taken into account when considering the motivations particular types of jobs and their occupants require.

2.1 Inside order taker/sales assistant

In this type of sales job there is a high degree of security and the minimum amount of ambiguity, e.g. the hours of work are fixed; customers

Table 2.1

Nine categories of sales job

Type of position	Sells	Job characteristics
1 Inside order taker/sales assistant	Usually serves behind a shop counter. Customers have made up their minds to buy, e.g. groceries, hardware. He serves them; he may suggest alternatives	Little opportunity for creative selling but may trade-up choice; main job requirements are to be reliable, of good appearance and courteous
2 Van salesman	Mainly delivers food and non-food products, e.g. fuel oil, coal, laundry, soft drinks, milk, bread	Reliability. A pleasant manner and good service are more important than aggressive selling. Few do any creative selling
3 Manufacturer's salesman calling on retail trade	Sell food and non-food products to shops, supermarkets, cash and carry, e.g. detergents, hardware, food, books	Mostly repeat selling; a pleasant manner, good service and reliable to follow a regular journey cycle; little scope for creative selling
4 Goodwill builder - 'missionary' salesman	Educates potential users of the product or users to widen or increase their use of it, e.g. pharmaceutical products to doctors, brewery representatives, and specifier's products (architects, engineers)	Usually cannot take orders but builds a climate of awareness in which the benefits of a specific product or service will be favourably considered when the need arises
5 Technical salesman	Sells electronic equipment, industrial products or highly engineered component parts to original equip-	Major emphasis is his technical know-how. Often too preoccupied with technical details; tends to forget his job is

Type of position	Sells	Job characteristics
	ment manufacturers	to sell. Far better to employ someone who can sell than an engineer who might or might not
6 Creative speciality salesman (of 'tangibles')	Sells consumer durables that are often desirable but not essential, e.g. washing machines, cars and educational books	Has to make the prospective customer dissatisfied with existing product or situation before he can begin to sell his product. This requires a highly structured selling presentation and he is a salesman who faces many refusals; a sales job often truly described as 'hard' selling
7 Creative speciality salesman (of 'intangibles')	Sells intangibles which are often desirable but not essential to life, e.g. advertising space, life assurance, stocks and shares, incentive schemes and banking services	Usually more difficult than the previous category because the product is less readily dramatised; its benefits come later or are difficult to comprehend. A very hard selling job requiring persistence and a highly structured approach
8 Political or indirect salesman	Sells products or services to large users: fuel-oil contracts, flour to bakeries, cement to local authorities, chemical aggregates such as sand, gravel, etc.	Usually little or no differences between competing products or services offered. The salesman only has himself to be better at looking after the needs of the buyer; he is a wheeler-dealer, sometimes a skilled negotia-

Type of position	Sells	Job characteristics
		tor, and sometimes a politician
9 Multiple salesman	Sells products or services to groups of people such as committees, boards of directors, project teams of engineers, e.g. computers and technological products for defence equipment, research, consulting services, pension schemes and merchant banking	The most difficult and skilled selling job; the salesman usually makes presentations to several people with different rather than similar needs. Usually more people say 'no' to his schemes than say 'yes'. He must have presence, charm and a highly developed empathy

Notes

Categories 1 to 5 are usually highly structured in every aspect of the sales job, e.g. who is to see or is seen, what to do and how to do it, the procedure for completing sales administration.

Categories 6 and 7 are much less structured yet need to be to combat the high number of refusals which reduce the cutting edge of selling skill.

Categories 8 and 9 are very little structured. Also very few people are qualified to do this sort of selling succesfully. That is why, as a rule, they earn a lot of money.

usually have made up their minds what they want to buy so that the salesman's job is more to serve and possibly select/suggest an alternative rather than to have to persuade; merchandise is pre-priced, sales procedures are defined very precisely in a manual; pay, whilst not as attractive as in some selling jobs, does not fluctuate violently although bonus or commission can sometimes be earned on special lines of goods. Such jobs will not appeal to the status seeker although the need for status has frequently been the motivating force that has led men and women to work in some of the most prestigious shops and salons in many capital cities such as London, New York, Paris, Rome and Zurich.

2.2 Van salesman

Many of the motivational factors relating to category 1 apply also to the van salesman. This job is normally highly structured with defined journeys and tasks each day. One element of the job highlights the need for security and to belong. A van salesman, although calling each week on a large number of customers, is on his own for a large proportion of each day.

2.3 Manufacturer's salesman calling on retail trade

This category of sales job is also well defined with laid down journey cycles and procedures governing most elements of the selling activity. Whilst historically this type of selling has been reasonably secure with a high ratio of orders to calls made, takeovers and mergers can overnight remove a salesman's independent buying point and turn it into a branch with a restricted buying list. The sales job then either disappears or becomes a merchandising activity rather than a selling one, which is easier but results in loss of status.

2.4 Goodwill builder - missionary salesman

Because of the inconclusive relationship that invariably exists between this type of selling and the customer, salesmen frequently feel insecure through lack of tangible orders and so need a lot of supportive management. The need for self-confidence and status building is high for those sales jobs where the customer is a professionally qualified man or woman and the information to be conveyed must be accurate as well as persuasive, e.g. architects, dentists, doctors, engineers.

2.5   Technical salesman

This type of sales job is a magnet for technical perfectionists and 'professionally qualified' engineers etc. who with reluctance include the word 'sales' in their titles. For the sales manager the motivational implications of this type of job are quite complex: the status of being at one with his professional customers can be counterproductive to sales results; similarly the desire to satisfy the need for perfection can also be costly in time and sales results.

2.6   Creative speciality salesman (of tangibles)
2.7   Creative speciality salesman (of intangibles)

These two categories of sales jobs attract salesmen who usually have a pronounced need for money. The commission element in every sale is attractive but the ratio of orders to calls is very low. In some instances such as selling insurance and financial incentive schemes thirty calls have to be made to obtain one or two sales. This high level of rejection is insupportable to the normal person so salesmen who can tolerate it and succeed in this environment are often somewhat neurotic. Whilst resenting it, they need the motivational security of firm, structured almost autocratic management and discipline. In fact they are much happier managed autocratically to compensate for the threatening, insecure atmosphere in which they are selling.

2.8   Political or indirect salesman
2.9   Multiple salesman

The comments about categories 6 and 7 apply to an even greater extent to these last two. Category 9 type sales jobs are financially very highly rewarded and the amount of job security is correspondingly low. Because so many of the decisions are reached by groups of people sitting as buying committees, such salesmen live in an environment in which, whilst a number of people can say 'no', only one can say 'yes'. Their propositions can be rejected by the negatives of what they may regard as functionary clerks. This arouses not only resentment but a renewed desire to win at all costs. So the need to compete is deeply embedded in their make-up.

2.10 Difficulties of the sales job

Selling is a social skill and salesmen are employed to use it day in and day out to persuade customers and prospects to part with their own or their firm's money in exchange for products, services or ideas.

Maintaining this persuasive skill at the level needed to succeed is very difficult for the following reasons:

1 In nearly every selling situation from the simple purchase of a loaf of bread to complicated and important decisions involving large sums of money such as buying a car or a computer, customers invariably have a choice of at least two alternative sources of supply.

2 This freedom of customer choice means that one company's salesman is going to face the refusal of his proposition in favour of a competitor's offering. This sales situation is socially an unnatural one in which to spend a major part of one's working life.

3 Such customer refusals and rejections are frequent for salesmen selling products or services which may be desirable but are not essential or where there are many competing companies offering almost identical products such as banking and insurance, cars, double glazing, advertising. These customer refusals and rejections result in the sharpness of selling technique being eroded leading to fewer sales, loss of self-confidence and morale.

4 Normally the great majority of salesmen are geographically spread. They work from home and spend the greater part of their working lives - on average 80-90 per cent - in unsupervised situations. Bearing in mind the problems of customer rejections, this socially lonely existence causes problems of communication, motivation and control.

5 Those who choose selling as an occupation are usually the least equipped to cope with strains that go with it. Selling attracts many men who have failed in their first choice of career either through lack of opportunity or of application to pass the necessary examinations. Such men often need *constant, strong, leadership* yet the very nature of the sales job makes it difficult to supply.

These five problems present you as a sales manager with some formidable challenges. You have to recognise the importance of spending as much time as you can out on the job with each salesman repairing eroded morale and selling technique through effective individual training and development. This is so important that I have written a workbook devoted entirely to it.[1] But your success in training and above all motivating your salesmen to succeed will hinge as much as anything else upon the leadership you give.

2.11 Motivation and leadership style

In recent years there has been a deluge of theories and papers about styles of leadership. The subject also produces an inevitable conflict in management circles as to which is the most appropriate style for salesmen.

The dispute turns upon which of two opposed theories is preferable.

1 *The autocratic-dictatorship philosophy* in which there are no grey areas. Everything is spelt out in terms of what management wants done. It assumes (on the McGregor Theory X basis) that salesmen are by nature indolent and irresponsible and need tight structure and control to be productive. Communication is one way from management and opinions are not sought or asked for.

2 *The democratic-participative philosophy* (based on Theory Y) which assumes that salesmen are creative, imaginative, seeking responsibility and desiring self-fulfilment.

In reality neither style is valid and these two extremes are caricatures or laboratory management models. Few managers today are absolute autocrats. Conversely only under special circumstances and with limited numbers of personnel is the democratic-participative style practical. Winston Churchill is said to have remarked that democracy was the worst form of government until you looked at the alternative (implying a dictatorship). Yet there are few countries or companies that are ruled by truly/purely democratic philosophies.

No single philosophy nor one style of leadership is applicable to all the situations you will be called upon to resolve or to the varied types of people your sales force contains.

Leadership and styles are as varied as the people who are subjected to them, ranging at one extreme from no supervision at all (laissez-faire) to absolute dictatorship at the other.

Five distinct styles can be distinguished (see Figure 2.1):

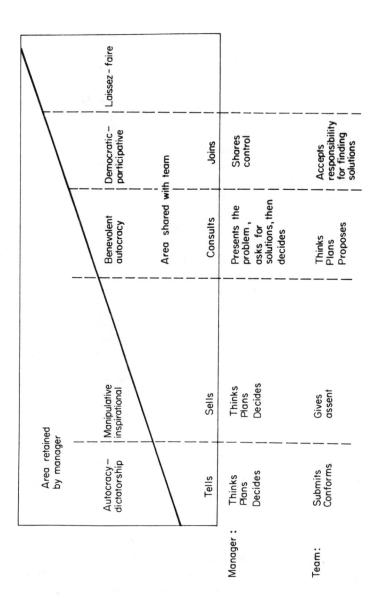

Fig. 2.1 Styles of leadership

Autocracy-dictatorship. Here the activities of the group are totally, arbitrarily and rigidly defined and structured. Management does not want or seek any participation by members of the group in reaching decisions which concern them. The role of the manager is similar to that of his military counterpart demanding unquestioning obedience at all times. Interestingly some of the most successful business tycoons are dictators. But their success depends upon knowing every aspect of the market and of their own operations. In today's complex marketing environment few can claim to be in such God-like command and control of all the elements of a business except very small ones. Moreover such a style of leadership is unacceptable to the majority of people working in commerce and industry today. Even so, there are times when it is better to be an impartial dictator than a popular failure.

A retired railway signalman told me that in the days of steam locomotives his own dictatorial style of managing the family saved his son's life when the lad was seven years old. His signal box was on one side of the main line near Peterborough on which the old *Flying Scotsman* train from London to Edinburgh used to travel at speeds approaching 100 m.p.h. He lived in a railway house on the opposite side of the track from the signal box. On holidays when no trains were due to pass through the section, his son on a word of command from his father would walk across the line and deliver his luncheon box.

One day, after the little boy had started across the line, an unscheduled express train came hurtling into view for no accountable reason. Realising that his son could not reach either side of the track and safety in time, the signalman barked out in a loud voice, 'lie down flat between the railway lines where you are at once.' Immediately his son did as he was told, the train shot through the section and over his son and disappeared into the distance. A little dazed and dusty but otherwise unharmed, the boy got to his feet and finished his interrupted journey to the signal box.

I remember so well the railwayman's final comments. 'Nowadays with youth questioning everything their parents say I suppose if I said to a youngster in the same situation what I said to my son he'd start arguing "why should I?"'

Manipulative, inspirational style. Here the approach is based on the philosophy of 'sell 'em', on doing the job and will be familiar to salesmen. The group has structure; targets and standards are imposed by management with little sales force participation. Salesman acceptance of these targets, standards and methods is achieved by subtle manipulative arm bending, inspirational sales conferences, and efforts directed at 'selling' compliance. The manager leads the group with varying degrees of authoritativeness, e.g. 'Bill, about this increased target. You say it is impossible. Yet Harry, who is not half the salesman you are, reckons he can do it. So what about it, Bill?'

Benevolent autocracy. Here the management is usually authoritarian and decisive but benevolent in seeking the positive participation of its staff in the decisions that are reached. The group's activities are usually partially or largely structured, and supervision is relatively close and unambiguous.

Salesmen are encouraged to make suggestions about the key decisions affecting their work such as realistic sales targets, numbers of calls to be made, types of business to be developed, training needed etc. In the light of their comments management decides upon a course of action which may reflect some, all or none of the ideas fed to it. But the act of genuine, sincere *consultation* provides a positive environment wherein there tends to be creativity and the taking of calculated risks; ideas are explored and innovative approaches are encouraged. Unlike the democratic approach, however, final decisions are reserved for the manager.

Democratic-participative. Here the management provides some structure and framework within which work is carried out. But within this framework the manager puts to the group all the decisions that have to be made. The group then arrives, by a process of majority choice, at decisions, usually the least risky of those open to them. The choice becomes the management's decision. The manager *joins* the group acting primarily as an adviser with a minimum of authority. Often called committee or bottom-up style of management, it approximates to the ideal of involvement, participation and what 'good' democratic society is about. But from a business viewpoint the dangers are that decisions tend to be long, drawn-out, conservative in character and often an unsatisfactory compromise to please the majority and gain its support. You can nevertheless use this approach most effectively when it is essential for all in the group to be fully committed to a line of action, or when management is not so much concerned what decision is reached so long as some conclusion or view is reached. The practice of democracy in these circumstances is not only appropriate but has high incentive value to the group.

A good example of the effectiveness of this approach concerns a major confectionery and food group which was about to replace its entire fleet of vehicles. Hitherto the specifications had been agreed at board level with the inevitable niggles by the drivers and van salesmen and subsequent fault-finding and indifference to maintenance schedules. Management decided to delegate the decision and recommendation as to the most suitable vehicle within certain legal and price limitations to the drivers. As a result of the vehicle 'we chose' the drivers and van salesmen have a personal identity with the fleet. It is being maintained better than ever before, and loss of sales through breakdowns has been reduced.

Laissez-faire. Here the group is given no structure or supervision at all. Its members set their own goals, pace and standards of performance. The manager or leader rarely has any authority. He is simply *primus inter pares* (first among equals), comparable to a departmental head at a university. In my experience of sales organisations where it has been tried it has failed totally mainly for the reasons already given about the nature of most selling jobs. Even so, quite a number of young men and women coming into new areas of industry from universities flirt with this style when first promoted into management.

In practice few managers who are successful exhibit styles of leadership which conform precisely to one or other of these categories. Most provide a mix of two or more in varying degrees. Since the whole purpose of leadership is to lead a united group to achieve a common objective, the style adopted depends upon the manager and those he manages, the demands of the selling job performed, the character of the salesmen, and the manager's own personality, standards and expectations.

In the final analysis the choice of a specific leadership style will depend on each salesman's individual make-up, for example:

Salesman *A*. If he is strongly aggressive, selfish and emotionally immature or neurotic, he will need very firm, even nakedly dictatorial, supervision.

Salesman *B*. If he is rather passive, dependent and security oriented, he will be both more comfortable and productive under a benevolent autocrat.

Salesman *C*. If he is mature, self-reliant and emotionally well adjusted, he will respond well to democratic-participative, even laissez-faire management.

Figure 2.2 illustrates the ideas involved.

Some detailed notes on leadership will be found in the Appendix on page 121.

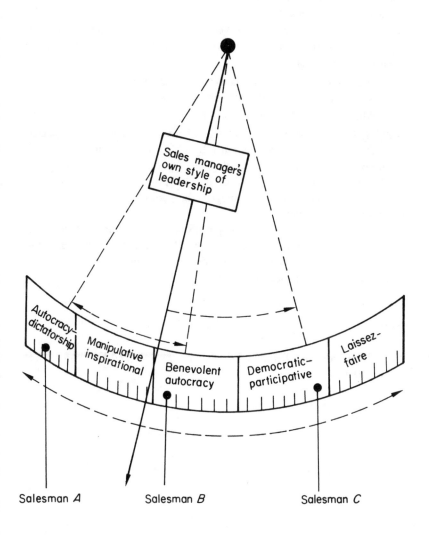

Fig. 2.2   Leadership relationship between sales manager and salesmen

Conclusion

The management and leadership of salesmen particularly at field first line level requires unusual skill. Salesmen want a leader they can respect. He does not have to be popular. Indeed any manager who courts popularity cannot manage because he will find it almost impossible to take the right but often unpopular decisions that are inseparable from the management task:

1 Critical appraisal of performance when necessary.
2 Responsibility for mistakes of subordinates.
3 Dismissal of unsatisfactory salesmen.

Nothing I have said implies that an effective manager is an unprincipled chameleon. Although he must be able to adapt himself to each separate situation and apply the degree of autocracy or permissiveness needed to achieve disciplined results, he pivots from his own well defined standards of personal integrity but does not sacrifice them on the altar of expediency.

'As for the best leaders, the people do not notice their existence. The next best, the people honour and praise. The next, the people fear; and the next, the people hate.... When the best leader's work is done the people say, we did it ourselves.' (Lao-tzu)

Note

[1] John Lidstone, *Training Salesmen on the Job* (2nd Edition), Gower Press, 1986.

3 Financial incentives

Money, one of the basic means by which a company first attracts a salesman to join its sales force and then rewards him for his efforts as well as
retaining his services, is the subject of endless debate among sales
managers. But despite the constant stream of articles, books and
reports about the relative importance of money for rewarding or modifying the direction of people's efforts at work, very few facts have been
presented about how it works. Money, this familiar tangible thing,
must then be used in a way we really don't understand, to help to make a
group of individuals achieve a particular goal. In the wake of Herzberg's widely publicised theories it became fashionable to disparage the
quest for money and to say that individuals work for much more important things in life. Every sales manager looks for the 'right remuneration
system' to unlock the door to total commitment. Yet how many companies are investing any time and funds in research to find out which
method of remuneration - straight salary, salary plus commission on
sales, commission only, straight salary at first and then moving to commission etc. - produces the most profit? Over the last fifteen years I
know of only two companies that have studied this question in depth:
one in the USA took four years to complete; the other in the UK took
eighteen months. Most sales forces are paid by arbitrary and unproven
methods of remuneration. Nevertheless there are a number of things we
do know which we can take into account and thus improve the results of
payment policies in such areas as:

1 How important is pay?
2 Establishing salary levels.
3 Conditions in which payment by results works.
4 Uselessness of annual bonuses as motivators.
5 Importance of publishing company salary scales.

3.1 Importance of pay

Whilst pay is relatively important to everyone who works there are
three conditions in which it is vital.

1 *When pay is below subsistence level.* In the UK this is rare. Even the
unemployed are cushioned from the worst effects of poverty by social
security payments and supplementary allowances. But there are many

salesmen and saleswomen working overseas where the level of pay is so low that the individual's whole being is concentrated on obtaining more money to satisfy the basic physiological needs. As international companies expand their operations into all parts of the world more thought should be given to this factor. Where employees' pay is below or at bare subsistence level 'moonlighting', the practice of doing another job at night besides one's main employment, is common in many countries in Africa, South East Asia, the Caribbean and South America. Its impact on the quality and quantity of work done during the day can be considerable and costly.

2 Pay preoccupies a person to the exclusion of all else *when it is below his habitual living standards*. Everyone needs a certain minimum level of income to pay for his normal expenses such as the rent on a flat or mortgage repayments, food, lighting and clothing, the cost of school meals or school fees etc. Obviously individual needs vary. A single man or woman generally does not need the same as a married man with three children. Yet marriage or suddenly having to take on the financial burden of housing and looking after elderly parents can render his take home pay totally inadequate. This is why it is so important for sales managers to assess the financial situation thoroughly when candidates are initially interviewed for a sales job. Many salesmen have been tempted to join companies offering total take home pay that superficially appears an improvement upon their existing insufficient remuneration. But they discover that they have jumped out of the frying pan into the fire. Their basic salary is no better than before. They can only close the gap between what they need to support their increased living standards and their basic pay by means of commission which may be impossible to earn or is quite insufficient.

3 *When pay is seen or thought to be unfair.* Nothing causes more resentment than the discovery or (unfounded) belief that another salesman for reasons other than competence is earning more money than you are especially if you know that his sales results are not as good as yours. Apart from the Civil Service and a few companies where salary scales are published, individuals can be remarkably dishonest about what they are actually paid. Here are two of many examples I know illustrating this human propensity to dissemble and to exaggerate.

During a discussion on communications, a group of senior salesmen, all attending an in-company one-week residential training course, were asked to write down on a piece of paper what they thought the person sitting next to them was paid. Not one of the twelve answers was correct to within £200.

At the end of my first year as a salesman in a subsidiary of the then

Shell-Mex and BP I was bidden to the divisional annual sales conference. In addition to the normal things that happen on these occasions, it was customary for the divisional manager to hand each salesman a sealed envelope. In this was a note to say if you had been given a rise and how much it would be. In my first envelope I learned that I had been awarded a rise of £35 per annum. Now although I am talking about over twenty-five years ago I still thought it quite inadequate and said so in no uncertain terms in that favourite debating chamber, the men's lavatory. Turning to a colleague I said, 'What rise did you get, Freddie?' 'A miserable £90' was the reply.

Funny, I thought Freddie's published sales figures for the year in percentage and in any other terms were not as good as mine. Then I asked another salesman what he received. He told me he had *only* got £120. Two men with sales results that did not compare with mine had both got rises dramatically greater than mine. You can imagine the state of bloody-mindedness and demotivation in which I departed from that sales conference.

Many years later when I was promoted into a management position I looked up the files for that first year to see what rises were actually given to that twelve-man sales team. Only four salesmen including me had been awarded rises and all exactly the same - £35. And the two who had said they had got £90 and £120? They had had no rises at all that year!

Publishing in-company salary scales in each year's sales plans eliminates a great deal of the suspicion many salesmen harbour that some men are more equal than others or that newer entries have been taken on to the pay roll at starting salaries higher than those paid to some of the longest serving men. If a company's salary scales have to be increased to attract the calibre of candidate needed, then the salaries of the entire sales force should be adjusted at the same time. Otherwise the resentment caused when the bush telegraph starts working will lose the company more goodwill and sales than the cost of giving the increases. Here, as in so many other areas of motivation, it is not too difficult to forecast human reaction and so avoid a decision which will create wholesale disenchantment with management and damage to morale.

3.2 Establishing salary levels

To avoid this happening, a company should have a clearly defined remuneration policy which would help achieve at least the following objectives:

    1   To attract sales personnel of the right calibre.

2　To encourage sales personnel to achieve their job objectives.
3　To reward sales personnel in accordance with the value of their contribution.
4　To prevent loss of morale through dissatisfaction with levels of pay.
5　To encourage sales personnel to stay with the company if it is in their own and the company's best interests.
6　To enable sales personnel to move up or across departmental, divisional or company boundaries (where a company is part of a group).
7　To achieve these aims at minimum cost.

Many organisations who pay their salesmen wholly or mainly by straight salary have developed salary scales based upon job grades, because of the worth and contribution to the company's business objectives of such remuneration and not least its market value. This is the first step in creating a salary policy. Once such a scale has been created the company can reward individuals for their performance. A trainee salesman on joining would start on the bottom of the scale while learning the job and progress up the scale as he meets and achieves the key sales targets and other job objectives set within the timetable laid down.

The second step is establishing precise standards against which individual sales performance can be measured, so that position on the salary scale can be determined on an objective basis.

These standards, agreed with the salesmen at the start of the sales year on which salary movements are based, enable a systematic and fair appraisal of performance to be carried out. It also prevents management from giving rises for reasons other than merit. Two factors only should govern salary and salary movements: the *amount* of a salary should be based upon the *responsibility* the job carries and *rises* given should be based upon the *competence* with which that responsibility is discharged.

There are other characteristics which an effective salary policy and structure should have and which will be expanded upon in the chapter on job satisfaction. These are:

1　Salary scales for jobs to which salesmen are eligible for promotion or transfer should be published, e.g. those of sales training officer, first and second line sales management and the various grades of product and marketing management to motivate the ambitious.
2　The existence and knowledge of these rising series of salary ranges provides ladders of growth and motivation.

3   There should be a sufficient span between minimum and maximum salary to accommodate a wide variety of sales performance and to motivate those who do not want promotion but who do want to see growth in their salaries to reflect their sales contribution and value to the company.
4   There should be a sufficient overlap between sales and management grades so that a top class salesman within the salesman salary range is paid more and is seen to be temporarily more valuable to the company than an inexperienced first line manager starting in a higher salary range.
5   The differentials between ranges should not be so close as to demand frequent reassessments of jobs; nor should they be so far apart that injustice is done when jobs are assessed on the borderline between one salary range and the one immediately above it.

Figure 3.1 shows these ranges as a model.

3.3   Conditions necessary for the operation of payment by results

Apart from payment by straight salary, many companies reward salesmen on a payment by results basis.

Over the last decade published surveys have shown that the number of companies paying by commission only is declining rapidly. This reflects the difficulty companies experience in recruiting sufficient candidates of the right calibre who are prepared to work for commission only. In addition a large majority of salesmen prefer the security of having a major proportion of their remuneration assured each month.

The main payment by results schemes operated by companies and their advantages and disadvantages appear to be as follows.

Commission only
This is used mainly in speciality selling where competition is fierce and sales can only be achieved by sustained personal selling, e.g. educational books, life assurance, office supplies and equipment etc.

Advantages
  (a)   attracts at the best level self-sufficient salesmen,
  (b)   reduces administration and sales overheads,
  (c)   makes allocation of rewards fair,
  (d)   no argument or doubts,
  (e)   incentives are simple and maximum per unit sale.

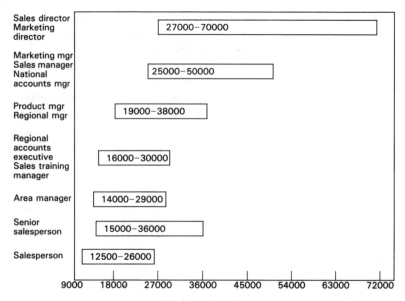

Fig. 3.1 Sales force positions and salary grades (based on *Sales and Marketing Rewards Survey 1993–1994*, by permission of Reward Group for Chartered Institute of Marketing)

Disadvantages

(a) salesmen only concerned with the sale that earns commission,
(b) servicing and follow-up suffers,
(c) pressure to earn money leads to 'hard' selling and sometimes making spurious claims for a product's performance which cannot be substantiated,
(d) absence of job security,
(e) high staff turnover.

Salary plus commission on sales

This is one of the most popular of schemes used by companies in a wide variety of industries.

Advantages

(a) is flexible and can be tailored to suit a particular market or to direct sales effort to specific products,
(b) basic salary satisfies salesman's need for security,

34

(c) commission is tangible evidence of success and a means of rewarding extra effort,

(d) provided it is planned with care, can be simply administered.

Disadvantages

(a) difficulty of establishing the correct mix of salary and commission can lead to complications and complicated schemes,

(b) short term volume/market pressures can lead to managers meddling with scheme and making it unbalanced or unfair.

Salary plus bonus

These schemes are normally of two kinds, individual or group. Sometimes bonus schemes are used as topping up additions to salary plus commission. They are often used by companies as a means of double insurance when launching a new product or a re-launched one; or when special activities are required in addition to normal sales work such as recruiting new outlets etc.

Advantages

(a) enables special efforts to be rewarded over and above achieving sales targets, e.g. servicing calls and following up leads,

(b) administrative efficiency such as maintaining accurate and up-to-date customer record cards,

(c) maintaining cash flow by keeping outstanding customer accounts within defined limits etc.

Disadvantages

(a) tendency by companies to delay bonus payments until they are dissociated from particular effort or desired result, leading to dilution of effort,

(b) standard bonuses unrelated to sales effort seen as a right and taken for granted,

(c) group bonuses do not motivate the individual because of lack of identity with individual effort.

There are six preconditions which must be met for a payments by results scheme to operate successfully.

1 *The sales results produced from a sales territory should be directly related to the efforts of each salesman.*

If other factors play a major part in contributing to the sales target such as heavy promotional expenditure, loss of orders due to production hold-ups or an industrial dispute, then it is difficult if not unfair for a

35

part of a salesman's total remuneration to depend upon commission.

2 *Sales results from a sales territory should be related solely to the individual efforts of the salesman over which he has control.*
In more and more sales situations the factors that influence the final purchase decision are not only complex but involve a number of people. This applies to other areas than national accounts in the grocery and fast moving consumer markets as the following examples illustrate.

To support the sales force activity a company in the radio communications market advertised its product in business magazines. The chairman of a company decided on the spur of the moment to have this system installed in all his lorries. He sent the order, worth over £300,000, to the company's head office. It so happened that commission at the rate of ten per cent was paid to the salesman in whose area orders originated. In this particular instance the salesman in question had never called on the firm placing the order. In another case a pharmaceutical company decided to pay commission on the sales of a newly launched product that could only be obtained on prescription. By chance or design the product was mentioned in passing on a BBC radio phone-in programme compered by a well known disc jockey. The woman phoning in said it had done wonders for her arthritis. The result of this gratuitous plug was a perpendicular leap in sales of this product. On paper salesmen almost doubled their salaries in commission. The only snag was that the company tried to wriggle out of paying on the grounds that the sales after this broadcast had been due to factors other than individual sales efforts.

Where commission earned cannot be fairly identified as due to one individual salesman's efforts then any arbitrary share-out between two or more people, all with claims to a slice of the cake, will only lead to dissatisfaction. So far as the pharmaceutical industry is concerned the accumulated evidence about prescription medicines suggests that no commission experiments have worked satisfactorily.

3 *There should be a large number of orders throughout the sales year to which the payment by results scheme is geared.*
If a salesman is paid solely or mainly by commission then it is essential for his own financial management to have an even flow of commission earnings throughout the year. In the capital goods market, for example, if by a quirk of chance he relied for his commission on one or two major orders and he did not secure them until halfway through the sales year, considerable financial hardship could result.

Alternatively salesmen in another market could earn the bulk of their commission early in the year and not bother for the remainder of the time. This happened to a company selling products direct to the general public via a commission only sales force that received twenty-five per cent of the purchase price of each item sold. Prices ranged from £5 to £300 with an average unit price of £50.

Every year in March the company took a stand at the Ideal Home Exhibition. It was staffed by the top five salesmen in the previous sales year. This was considered a major reward because during the period of the exhibition about 1,200 orders would be taken by these five salesmen, earning them each about £3,000 in two weeks.

These five salesmen then used to take two or three months off because their financial needs had been satisfied for that period. *Commission will only motivate a salesman to work until he reaches the ceiling of his financial needs. Then he stops working.*

4 *The financial incentive should be realistic and high enough to reward extra effort and achievement.*

This is a major stumbling block in countries with a high rate of income tax such as the UK. Hence the growing attraction of awards in kind, and other forms of direct incentive.

5 *The system should be simple to understand and fair.*

A payment by results scheme that is complex and difficult to understand will inevitably be self-defeating in the same way that customers do not buy products or services whose benefits they cannot easily see and comprehend or relate to their needs.

Similarly where sales territories differ in terms of geography or sales potential such factors must be carefully weighted so that one salesman does not have an unfair advantage over another.

6 *The lapse in time between earning commission and being paid it should be as short as possible.*

There is an interesting law of learning involved here called the Law of Contiguity which states that people learn faster if effort expended on doing something is rewarded as soon as possible. The longer the gap between the effort put into earning commission and actually receiving the money the less the relationship between the two is seen and incentive is diminished. As Dryden very aptly put it:

> For present joys are more to flesh and blood
> Than the dull prospect of a distant good.

This is why annual bonuses are useless as financial incentives. It is difficult at the end of December to relate back across the previous twelve months to all the activities good bad and indifferent that went to produce the amount of bonus paid out.

Earlier in this chapter I referred to the lack of research into the outcomes that different payment by results schemes produce. The information yielded by the two major studies known to me are of interest. One carried out in the UK by an office equipment manufacturer sought to identify the *key* motivation(s) of the company's top twenty per cent salesmen both past and present measured in terms of sales results against a set of criteria. The reason for the research was the company's swing away from a largely commission only sales force towards one which, though still paid commission, had moved towards an element of straight salary, company cars and a number of other fringe benefits.

At the completion of an eighteen-month study, the evidence indicated that the best salesmen were only interested in money. This was the reason given by most of the salesmen who left the company.

The other and much larger study was carried out in America over a period of four years and concerned the selling of construction machinery and equipment through a country-wide network of dealership. The similar nature of the products sold enabled realistic comparisons to be made between salesmen selling the same products to similar outlets, motivated by a range of remuneration systems which embraced the following:

1 Straight salary alone
2 Salary and commission on total sales
3 Salary and commission on gross profit of salesman's total dollar sales
4 Straight salary and bonus
5 Straight salary, commission on total sales and bonus
6 Commission only on gross profit of salesman's total dollar sales
7 Straight salary and commission based on a sales quota
8 Commission only on total sales
9 Straight salary, commission based on a sales quota and bonus.

The results of this study produced the following conclusions:

1 Straight commission produced the largest sales volume but cost the most.
2 Salary and commission on total sales produced the second highest volume but produced the highest net profit.
3 Straight salary alone produced the least, yet cost the most in terms of sales volume.
4 The highest remunerated salesman earned three times more than the lowest paid but on average sold five times as much.

So far as I know no equivalent study has been carried out in the UK but there is no reason to believe that the findings here would differ much.

When the size of the wages bill for companies large or small is considered and the extent to which payment systems are currently rather a game of chance the following comment by Pigors and Myers [1] is apt:

> There are many wage incentive plans that are successful because the employers are carrying out the basic principle of consultation [and research] with their employees. The plan is working primarily because the employer has as a background the respect and loyalty of the employees. If this kind of relationship is lacking, it matters little how well worked out the plan is; it will fall short of the results expected of it.

Note

[1] Pigors, Paul and Myers, C.A., *Personnel Administration*, McGraw-Hill.

4 Direct incentives

Related to but distinct from basic remuneration and commission, direct incentives cover all the many and varied systems of payment - or 'benefits in kind', as the tax authorities term them - made to salesmen. These include fringe benefits, merchandise awards, points schemes, competitions, holiday incentives and 'salesman/saleswoman of the year' prizes.

4.1 Fringe benefits

Fringe benefits are benefits in kind paid for by an employer. Among the most common are sick pay, holidays, private use of a company car, luncheon allowances, pension and life assurance schemes, and membership, paid or partly paid by the company, of private medical schemes.

Generally speaking fringe benefits do not motivate in any consistent and measurable way. They tend to be regarded as either creating an environment in which salesmen are not unhappy or they make them feel more secure as in the case of pension schemes. Since company cars have so many status implications, I will deal with some direct incentive schemes using cars in a later chapter.

There is a plethora of companies offering incentive schemes to cater for every kind of need from gramophone records and clothing to glamorous holidays.

The success of all direct sales incentive schemes hinges upon some fundamental principles which should be borne in mind:

1 The schemes must be selected to fit into an overall marketing plan and not decided on a random basis or as a hasty expedient to rescue a sliding sales campaign.
   This means that if it is thought an incentive scheme can help in a positive way then consultation with a selection of companies will need to take place several weeks before the start of the financial year.
2 Companies have found that to maintain sales force excitement and involvement, incentive based sales campaigns ideally should not last longer than three to four months.
3 The value of the gift (excluding holiday schemes) should normally be equivalent to about one week's salary.

4 Incentive schemes, like commission, should be simple to operate and easy to understand.
5 Incentive schemes must be identified with specific and measurable objectives to facilitate monitoring and control and to maintain momentum.
6 Each scheme should be well researched to ensure that the basis on which it will operate will be acceptable and thus motivate every salesman. Two examples illustrate the disasters that can result from failing to do this.

Example 1

A major industrial company with five sales forces tested the acceptability of an incentive scheme (based upon a gift catalogue) in one of them. The sales force liked the idea, a pilot scheme was run and it produced the required results. So the company decided to install the same scheme in the other four sales forces but did so without any prior consultation with the salesmen concerned. They resented this and the scheme imposed upon them. It failed so the company threw it out. A considerable loss in sales in the following year occurred in the one sales force where the scheme had worked.

Example 2

A printing company sales manager decided to give a motor mower as a prize to all salesmen who achieved a certain volume of new business throughout the year. It failed to produce the expected sales because one-third of the salesmen lived in flats! The scheme - as so often happens - was selected for the worst of all reasons: the sales manager wanted a new mower for himself and the supplying company had promised him one free in exchange for installing the incentive scheme and ordering a minimum quantity - in advance.

Under the following broad headings are details of some of the many incentive schemes currently available to companies.

4.2 Specially tailored incentive schemes

There are a great many companies who will tailor-make an incentive scheme for any client company, large or small. Some companies have set themselves up as specialists in motivational scheme design, some are in fact parts of major organisations such as Marks & Spencer.

Merchandise awards/points schemes

Most of these companies operate more or less along the same lines based on gift catalogues containing thousands of items of merchandise which appeal to every member of the salesperson's family. Potential gifts range from kitchen utensils, children's toys, garden tools, furniture to all ranges of sports equipment etc. The schemes are linked to some form of points system, designed to achieve specific sales objectives by each and every member of the sales force. The choice of gift(s) is governed by the number of points or credits a salesperson is awarded for his or her sales achievements. There are two obvious attractions to these schemes:

1 All members of the sales force can benefit and receive tangible gifts of their choice rather than the same 'top performers' always carrying off the big prizes.

2 The entire family is interested in the results of the breadwinner's sales performance because in many companies the family is sent a copy of the gift catalogue at the start of an incentive scheme.

Indeed, the overt encouragement and self-interest of the family is an integral part of the success of many such schemes.

4.3 Travel incentive schemes

In 1990, the value of the world-wide travel incentive market was $17 billion (£11 billion). It is estimated that by the end of this century the total will be $56 billion (£31 billion) Given the accuracy of this massive spend in one area alone of incentives, companies need to be aware of some of the guidelines, problems and pitfalls of travel incentive schemes.

Group travel incentive schemes

Group travel schemes are ideal for large company sales forces, dealerships and multi-branch networks of managers, e.g. large insurance companies, car manufacturers' dealerships, white goods chain stores. Such staff usually provide a captive audience for travel incentive marketing using videotapes and glossy brochure campaigns.

Individually tailored travel schemes

Individual travel schemes differ in many respects from group ones. So companies need to be clear about the purpose of the scheme in relation to the overall marketing and sales objectives, for example: how will the programme be budgeted?; who would qualify to go on the trip? The secret of their success is to set specific sales objectives which individuals believe are just about achievable.

4.4 Selecting or designing the best scheme

The following points are worth bearing in mind:

1 An incentive programme which limits participation to sales staff could be short-sighted as increased sales only actually materialize after processing staff, storemen, delivery drivers and the like have made their contribution.

2 Incentive planning must be based on detailed knowledge of the company's market-place, product/services range, people structure and salary packages.

3 Should research reveal a breakdown in communication between management and staff, the company may not be ready to launch a motivation programme; indeed, to do so may add insult to injury.

4 The full commitment of senior management is essential. If management aren't seen to be supporting the programme, the staff may well feel 'why should I?'.

5 The programme structure should ensure that extra revenue than planned is encouraged.

6 The programme should have a quantifiable bottom-line impact, for example:
   i)   a percentage increase over same period last year
   ii)   achieving sales target plus a given percentage
   iii) opening of a specific number of new accounts
   iv)   the total value of new business over budget
   v)   increased percentage of new points of sale over target.

7 If funds are tight, don't fall into the trap of offering a league-table structure with sales staff competing for a limited number of awards. Those at the lower end of the league may see the 'winners circle' as an impossible goal.

8 Targets must be achievable. However, sales targets which do not provide an opportunity to stretch performance do not generate the additional profit needed to pay for the programme.

9 A detailed post-mortem should be planned to follow each campaign to measure objectively the result achieved.

It has long been recognised that cash incentives beyond a certain level are losing their driving and motivating power, not least because apart from the tax element, money tends to become a part of the salesperson's salary. It loses in consequence its relationship with particular sales achievement, and certainly for a great many sales personnel does not register in the mind as forcibly as a tangible reward for effort which can be seen, admired and used or enjoyed.

For these reasons incentives in one form or another are here to stay. Most of the schemes and ideas tend to be variations on a common formula demonstrating in yet another area of business how much easier it is to imitate than to invent.

Sales managers in their search for new and imaginative ways of stimulating their sales forces to greater efforts should not overlook some of the less sophisticated methods that lie close at hand and are sometimes much more effective in their impact on sales performance.

One example is particularly relevant to export salespeople who spend weeks away from home living in impersonal hotels. In this era of 'spouse' half-price or even free air fares for frequent travellers, and hotels offering heavily discounted double room rates, the opportunity to take one's husband or wife on a sales tour once or twice a year and combine it with a short holiday is a powerful incentive that costs relatively little and has often proved a recipe for sales success in terms of new business obtained.

One thing is beyond dispute about all forms of sales incentive. Like products or services, they must be designed to meet and satisfy a need. Hunch is no substitute for research to assess whether a scheme will be acceptable and motivate or not. For example, an important item for everyone's annual budget is income tax. So if you plan an incentive scheme you need to be sure how it will be regarded by the tax authorities in your country, and its impact on each and every member of the sales force. The laws relating to what is and what is not a 'benefit in kind', and therefore subject to assessment for tax purposes, changes every year in the UK and therefore it would be pointless for me to attempt to define the current position. But generally speaking, since tangible incentives do not have a resale value, the tax liability on the individual recipient is usually a small one.

Each and every scheme you install has its advantages and disadvantages, but it is part of the art and science of management to use the most appropriate for the circumstance and the people involved. Incentives are *not* about rewarding people exceptionally for doing the sales job for which they are already paid a salary. To reward people over and above for doing what they are employed to do is, to say the least, curious. Incentive schemes should be reserved for that additional effort you ask of people that they are required to give beyond their normal day's work: that is the time to deploy incentives.

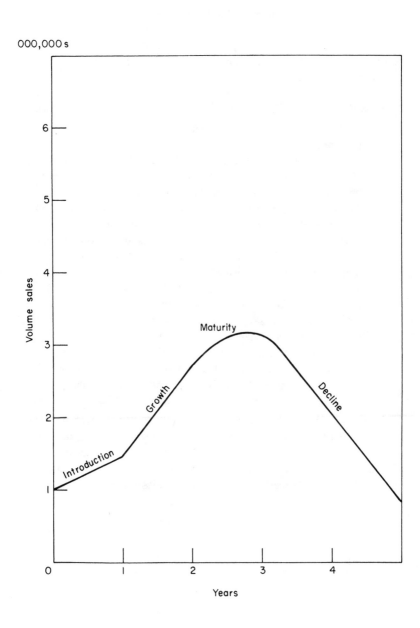

000,000 s

Volume sales

6 —

5 —

4 —

3 —   Maturity

                    Growth   Decline

2 —

   Introduction

1 —

0   1   2   3   4

Years

Fig. 4.1   Life cycle of sales force incentive schemes

4.5 Golden rules for all incentives schemes

Finally, in my experience, confirmed by countless managers who have reported their successes and failures to me, there are *two* golden rules to all incentive schemes.

First, incentives schemes, like products and human beings, have a life cycle as illustrated in Figure 4.1:

i) You have to carry out research to establish an acceptable programme.

ii) The incentive programme has to be *launched*, and during this phase of its life cycle the sales force has to be educated about the benefits it offers to them and what they must do to enjoy them.

iii) The incentive programme has a *growth* phase, during which the members of the sales force benefit from the rewards it offers.

iv) After a time, the scheme *matures* as a result of more and more people not only enjoying the benefits, but also broadcasting to other staff what they have got out of it.

v) Then, as in life and also with products and services, the scheme goes into *decline*. This is when, for example, a salesperson having once won, say, a holiday in Bermuda and enjoyed it, has since married and has a very young family. Surprisingly, or perhaps not, the prospect of another trip to the Caribbean islands does not appeal. And if it does not appeal, it does not motivate.

We are back with Maslow's fundamental discovery about human beings: *a satisfied motivation is not a motivator of human behaviour.*

My second golden rule applies when incentive schemes reach the stage of decline. This is *to scrap the incentive scheme* so that it does not act as a sales force *de*motivator. Start again, using as your guidelines the needs of your customers, the needs of the company and its shareholders, and last but by no means least, the needs of the sales force.

5 The need for security

Salesmen have a stronger need for security than any other group of people in commerce and industry. This stems back from the type of people who choose selling as a career and from the selling job itself.

Maslow identified security as a basic need whilst Herzberg found it to be most frequently a cause of dissatisfaction. Yet security is socially and psychologically a need which people are reluctant to acknowledge or speak about. It is rather like fear or cowardice or crying, things that men in particular will rarely admit, and so do not discuss openly with their managers.

Because of this reluctance to talk about security, it is often overlooked by managers or not given its due importance. It is all too easy for sales managers to forget those bouts of depression and insecurity they experienced as salesmen and only remember their successes. For their salesmen each day will have its quota of successes and failures - customer promises unfilfilled and downright rejections voiced in words of one syllable.

What makes a sales job intrinsically insecure?

5.1 Visibility of sales results

In very few jobs is the effectiveness of an employee's efforts as objectively visible and measurable as in that of the salesman in many areas of commerce and industry.

In some sales jobs there is the delayed shock when results lag far behind sales effort and day-to-day sales performance is subjectively rather than objectively measured as in selling to architects, doctors, engineers etc. - the kind of job categorised in Chapter 2 as 'missionary'.

When sales figures start to fall, it is the salesman's skill and ability that first come into question rather than any change in the market place or the competence of his manager. This contrasts markedly with the armed services where there are no bad soldiers, only bad officers. If a military campaign fails, it is to the officers first that blame is apportioned and from them that explanations are required.

When there is a doubt about the reasons for a shortfall in sales figures, managers all too rarely admit publicly that the fault may lie with them and the sales force is the last to get the benefit of any doubt.

5.2 Stress

Unlike office work many selling jobs have no fixed working hours. A combination of other elements makes it physically demanding: traveling by car day in and day out or continuously flying in cramped aircraft if you sell in overseas markets; the physical and psychological stress that builds up from spending the bulk of your working life with customers and prospects; the lack of frequent contact during the working week with colleagues and so very little opportunity to relax. Unlike the office worker who can lock up his desk at the end of a day's work, the salesman takes his work home with him.

Many of these influences are bound to result in diminishing performance as they take their cumulative toll.

5.3 Larger companies - fewer salesmen

The characteristics of the market place in which consumer, industrial and services sales forces work have been changed dramatically in the last few years by the emergence and growth of the big buyer. More and more markets are being dominated by companies larger in size but fewer in number. This development has led to a reduction in the size of sales forces in many companies and groups. Takeovers and mergers continue and the security of sales jobs is under constant threat.

5.4 Changing role of the sales force

The emergence of these large companies has increased the power and influence of their buyers. At the same time these buyers are becoming much more knowledgeable and well informed about the *products* and manufacturing *processes* of suppliers, *finance*, the art and skill of *negotiation* and also *marketing* and *selling*.

Unless the salesmen and saleswomen who do business with these buyers have comparable knowledge and skills in these areas their relationships will deteriorate and this can fuel feelings of insecurity.

5.5 Geographic separation from sales manager

Reference has already been made to the fact that the majority of salesmen work from home and that this causes problems of *communication*, *motivation* and *control.*

A person working in an office with his colleagues and boss has his perception of security increased when feedback about his performance is immediate and complete. By contrast the salesman's often extended physical and time separation from his manager results in feedback being limited and often delayed and so he is less likely than others to know where he stands. Ill considered memos which only communicate half the story sent from the office can add to a salesman's feeling of being on his own - succinctly expressed as, 'they don't tell me anything and when they do I am more confused than if they hadn't.'

5.6 Closeness to competition

It is fashionable and popular at sales conferences to refer in glowing terms to the sales force as 'our front line troops out in the battlefields of commerce.' But consider the underlying implications. Salesmen are the most likely to be aware - and aware first - of competitor performance and product improvements. These reactions are often emotional and biased rather than cool and detached. But who can blame them? They have been sent out to sell 'this product which is a marketing first; no one else is in the field' only to see an identical model on the shelves at the first call and cheaper than their own.

The salesman's feelings of security and belief in the superiority of his employers will hardly be strengthened by this type of competitive encounter, which is happening more and more frequently as the similarity between competing products increases.

All these factors will tend to increase the salesman's feeling of insecurity, raising in his mind questions about the present such as:

1   Can I hold down my job?
2   How am I doing in the eyes of the company?
3   Am I doing well enough?
4   Will my earnings be enough to pay this month's bills?

and in the future:

1   Will the company be taken over?
2   If so, what happens to my job?
3   Will I have a change of manager?
4   Will my pay suffer?
5   Can I keep up with the changes taking place?

5.7 Legislation to improve job security

In the majority of countries of the EEC and in many other countries, government legislation has been introduced to improve employee security. The most far-reaching in its impact in the UK is the Employment Protection Act.

Under this Act the employee is given a greater degree of protection than ever before in terms of minimum notice period; procedures governing job performance and grounds for dismissal; procedures for handling redundancies; training to equip employees to perform their jobs to standards required and in countless other areas.

It is not the purpose of this book to detail the ramifications of this and other acts of parliament which impinge upon our working life. But I do want to warn sales managers of the danger of assuming that the areas of insecurity to which I have referred have been dealt with by these laws. *The salesman's job still remains insecure because of the nature of the work.*

How then can you systematically help to meet your salesmen's need for security and either remove or diminish feelings of insecurity?

5.8 Provide clear objectives and standards

Clear job and sales objectives and standards of performance provide the essential framework a salesman must have so that he knows what for the company and his manager constitutes a satisfactory level of performance.

This begins at the selection interviewing stage when a candidate is told what the job is; the sales targets he would be expected to achieve, and the training he would be given to equip him to achieve them; the numbers of calls he will have to make to obtain a sale, etc. He should be told about the company's appraisal system and how it works.

Salesmen should be given clear and precise job descriptions which set out in detail:

1   Job title
2   Who salesman reports to
3   Specific job objectives
4   Duties and responsibilities of the job
5   How the job will be assessed e.g. sales calls to orders; expenses budget; type and frequency of appraisals etc.

Whilst salesmen should not be over-protected, knowing precisely what you are expected to do breeds confidence. Standards of performance are particularly important for 'missionary' selling jobs where no orders are taken and it is difficult to know on a daily basis if one's selling has been successful or not, e.g. selling to specifiers, the medical profession, those who influence decision making rather than the decision makers themselves.

5.9 Provide strong leadership

Salesmen need *constant, strong leadership* to counterbalance the morale- and confidence-eroding elements of their job. Yet by the very nature of the job, this need is difficult to supply. Sales managers must plan to accompany salesmen as frequently as possible and to give the kind of leadership that inspires confidence and respect. Guidelines on leadership have been given in Chapter 2.

5.10 Field accompaniment

But what about the frequency of your visits to individual salesmen in the field? Many sales managers make the mistake of devoting the majority of their time set aside for field visits to either their newest or weakest salesmen, leaving the so-called 'best' alone for long periods. Good salesmen feel just as lonely and insecure as bad ones; highly intelligent salesmen and saleswomen feel just as lonely as the less intelligent. So do those with academic qualifications.

As a general rule the tougher the sales job the more frequent supportive and field training visits should be. In pioneering sales jobs where the level of customer rejections will be high the need for security is considerable. In one company the first line managers speak to every one of their sales team at least once a day and accompany each one on an individual basis for one full working day in every five.

Half a day fitted in when you have time can often be more frustrating than not appearing at all. It is either perceived as a check-up to see if the salesman is doing his job, or, if he has a mind full of problems, you are unlikely to resolve them.

This need to spend time on the job with individual members of the sales force is overlooked by companies new to selling. I have in mind particularly the banking and financial services industry. Bankers now have to go out and actively sell their services - a new and for most of them an unnerving experience. *No one ever joined one of the major banks to become a salesman.* So the management has no current knowledge of the selling potential of its business developers nor of the cumulative effect of rejections of their propositions. As a result it is very rare that a banker is accompanied on his visits to sell to customers by his 'sales manager'. His selling skills are consequently likely to erode much more quickly.

So plan to spend as much time as you can with *all* your salesmen including the *best* in your team.

5.11 Satisfy the need to belong

Nearly all of us prefer to belong to a team or community rather than to be a lone wolf. Try to bring your sales team together as often as circumstances permit so that they feel part of a team and draw warmth and strength from being a part of it. A sales bulletin or sales letter circulated every week or month also helps to keep salesmen in touch. These communications, always started with the best intentions by many sales managers, fall too often by the wayside, sacrificed when work claims priority. To avoid this happening one company delegated the task of compiling a monthly sales letter to the salesmen - each member of the sales force doing it in rotation.

The insecurity felt by salesmen can be markedly decreased by the use of regular planned telephone conversations. The most effective structure for these conversations is as follows:

1. Ask each of your salesmen to telephone in at a set time each day or week, e.g. after the morning post has been opened and read or latest individual sales results are known to you.
2. Identify each salesman's achievements where possible, e.g. one or a series of successful sales or getting a meeting with a hitherto inaccessible prospect; identify major sales problems and your possible solutions.
3. Start the telephone conversation on a positive note congratulating if appropriate, then investigate his problems if he has any and give practical advice, reassure and encourage.
4. Always end the telephone conversation on a note of confidence and warmth.

This technique needs to be practised to work successfully. Remember that at the other end the salesman can only hear your words - he cannot see you. For sales forces involved in speciality selling where rejections are frequent or where there is lack of daily evidence of success, this technique is invaluable.

5.12 Avoid secrecy

Tell salesmen as much as you can about company policies, activities and personnel. One of the most pernicious contributions to salesman insecurity is the grapevine. There are many examples where companies are not deliberately secretive - just thoughtless. It does not help a salesman's morale if the first he hears about a new appointment in the marketing or sales department is when he opens his national daily newspaper and sees the advertisement. The following story illustrates this point.

On my way to lead a three-day conference of sales managers from a number of European chemical companies held in Amsterdam I saw in the appointments column of *The Financial Times* that one of the companies that was sending two delegates to it had made a number of management changes involving the chairman, managing director, and marketing director. At the coffee break on the first day of the conference I expressed great interest in these appointments only to discover that neither manager had heard about them. Furthermore both thought I had divulged private information. They were quite taken aback when I showed them that my source of information was nothing more sinister than a newspaper!

Morale is not increased if a customer starts discussing a new advertising campaign about which he, rather than the salesman, has been the first to be told. Tell salesmen bad news *first* and *fast* rather than let garbled versions of it leak out from head office or factory.

Time spent forecasting the effect on sales force morale of policy and organisational changes *before* such changes are announced is time well spent. The introduction of telephone selling by a national food and bottling company had considerable implications for the sales force. Among other changes salesmen had to give up certain specified personal accounts to the telephone sales girls and undertake new sales promotion activities. The sales force was deeply suspicious about this move because some of the older members recalled that another company had used telephone selling as a means of cutting the size of the sales force by twenty-five per cent.

When the reasons behind the policy were explained and it was realised that no jobs were at risk, the sales force co-operated fully in making this innovation a success.

5.13   Conclusion

The salesman's need for security is understandable when you remember the unnatural social relationship he has with his customers and pro- spects. Each day he has to persuade them to part with their own or their firm's money in exchange for his goods or services. These services more often than not are the same or only marginally different from those offered by competing firms. Coupled with the other five difficulties listed on page 21, the selling job brings with it elements of insecurity that are not common to other jobs. To provide you with a constant reminder of the need as a manager to increase feelings of security and to reduce the factors that produce insecurity, I have compiled the follow- ing checklist:

Security is	*Security is not*
clear orders	vague instructions
strong leadership	laissez faire - no leadership
firm structure	no objectives, no standards
belonging	no one to lean on
knowing	not knowing - secrecy

6 The need for status

Herzberg identified status as a hygiene factor in his theory on human motivation - as a potential source of dissatisfaction rather than as a positive motivator.

As we are all members of a society and of various social and working groups, we are very conscious and aware of our status within them. Or, as the dictionary defines status, 'of [our] relative standing, rank or position in society; [our] position in relation to others'.

The three main groups in which salesmen (indeed everyone) perceive their status are:

1 The *working group* - embracing customers as well as colleagues
2 The *social group*
3 The *family group*

In all three groups the individual must be able to stand tall psychologically. If his status in any one of these groups is threatened or diminished then he bleeds inside his mind. Of all the human motivations the need for status is probably the most difficult either to measure or to understand. The way it manifests itself often defies logic. In its more bizarre forms it can be amusing, offensive or pitiful.

A man I once interviewed told me of the traumatic effect on him of being made redundant. He could not bear the loss of dignity and status he imagined would follow telling his family. So for over a month he continued to leave home each day for 'work'. One can imagine the mental suffering of that man.

We start from a grave disadvantage if we judge everyone else's needs in this area against our own, using our own as some kind of yardstick of the normal balanced man.

The problem is that an individual's need for status is often something he will not openly discuss; often he is ashamed of it. And even when his needs are satisfied they are constantly being threatened. The loss of some status symbol can psychologically cause as much mental pain and suffering as the physical loss of an arm or leg.

Like other human needs, our need for status has its origins in childhood. Each child's needs develop as a result of his individual experiences. Cultural factors and relations with adults all go to fashion the pattern of motives that we take into adult life.

The clues to a person's need for status are not easy to find and assemble but we will identify them much more speedily if we try to comprehend such needs without being censorious either in our search or in what we discover.

Selling, as I have already mentioned, is for many a second or third choice of career because they did not have the academic capabilities of a clever brother or sister, or the opportunities.

A leading politician, ex cabinet minister and in monetary terms a millionaire, was the child of a working class family brought up in one of a long row of terraced houses. As a child he noticed that only one family in the street where he lived had a car. The breadwinner was an insurance salesman. So as soon as he was old enough to start earning a living he sought out a job in insurance spurred on by the one person who in his estimation had any tangible status in his street.

A salesman, hearing that his company was planning to enlarge the sales force and in consequence appoint four district sales managers, asked if he could be considered for one of these jobs. Not only this, he said that he would be quite prepared to take a reduction of £150 a year in his salary if appointed. Behind this example lies a status story that is far more common than you may realise. This salesman's wife was a demonstrator with a vacuum cleaner manufacturer and such a good one that they promoted her to be a sales supervisor. It was this change in the salesman's domestic situation that led him to offer to 'buy' a managerial job.

An advertising sales executive lived in the suburbs and travelled by train each day to his head office in central London. He was small in stature and, as a child and in later life, had a desperate need to be someone of consequence. His salary was insufficient to enable him to travel first class. Yet every day he entered a first class compartment when the train stopped at his station so that people on the platform would get the impression he could afford to travel in such style. He then walked down the train and sat in a second class compartment!

A famous company with shipping and oil interests in the City of London was renowned not only for the excellence of its directors' luncheons but also for the exclusiveness of its choice of guests who were invited to them. As a former First Lord of the Admiralty and prominent public figure, Sir Winston Churchill had never been invited to any of these luncheons and the fact rankled. On becoming Prime Minister in 1940 Sir Winston Churchill offered the chairman of this company a post in the Wartime Cabinet which he accepted. Sir Winston is said to have remarked when this new member of his Cabinet was about to take his leave 'and now Lord —— perhaps you will invite me to lunch in your boardroom'.

What can you do to satisfy the status needs of your sales force?

6.1 Satisfying status needs

1 *Management recognition of the importance of the sales force*

In a great number of companies the sales force carries the main burden and final responsibility for getting through to the customer and selling repeatedly. The sales force provides the spearhead of the company's marketing efforts. Yet too often senior management either fails to recognise this important role or merely goes through the motions of doing so. There are many steps that can be taken of which the following are some of the more obvious ones.

Role of the sales force in the company. When a salesman or saleswoman first joins the company a press release together with a photograph sent to the local papers will more often then not be inserted. This can help build up an individual's stature and job in the *social group* and community in which he lives. It will enhance his status in the *family* when they read about it. The same information can be included in a company magazine or newsletter so that the new member of the sales force is welcomed as an important and respected addition to the *work group*.

The rank and seniority of the manager who welcomes a new salesman on his first day also communicates the importance - or otherwise - of the salesman to the company. The managing director of a dairy equipment manufacturer always meets and welcomes every new member of the staff on the day they join.

Appreciation of the role of the sales force by non-marketing/sales staff. Short talks and appreciation seminars for non-marketing and non-sales staff can help to communicate throughout the company the contribution the sales force makes. This will both dispel many misconceptions and enhance the status of salesmen.

Field visits with salesmen by production and accountancy departmental staff will spread a better understanding of the nature and difficulties of the job. Too many people sitting comfortably in their warm offices on a bitterly cold day or in air cooled conditions on a swelteringly hot one are apt to make snide remarks about the salesmen 'swanning around the countryside wining and dining customers'.

2 *External symbols*

Unlike many of his colleagues in the office, the salesman has no office or desk, carpets or the other external symbols by which an individual's status may be assessed either by his colleagues or by his customers. He needs and looks for other external signs and symbols of his status in the company, with his customers and in the community. These can be conveyed and enhanced by:

1 The size and make of his car
2 His briefcase
3 His job title
4 His visiting cards
5 Symbols of successful performance (ties, special awards, etc)
6 Credit cards for business expenses
7 Club memberships

Job titles. Try to give your salesmen titles they can use without shame and which will be respected and not ridiculed. Contrast the appeal to the prospective candidate of a brewery who advertised for a 'free-trade sales executive' with another brewer that called its equivalent salesmen 'abroad clerks'; 'lingerie sales executive' with 'traveller in ladies' underwear'.

On the other hand beware of titles that can convey misleading impressions about a salesman's authority and responsibility. Nothing appeared so attractive or appealing to status to one company's sales force as the managing director's decision to call his salesmen 'directors'. Thus he had thereafter a 'sales director, Surrey', 'sales director, Yorkshire', and so on. This was splendid while customers bought at list prices, but when they wanted to negotiate and assumed they were dealing with a director with power to shave or amend prices, they found these so-called 'directors' had no delegated negotiating powers at all. Collapse of respect and status of the sales force in the eyes of the customers ensued.

Company cars. Cars supplied to salesmen and saleswomen as a working tool to enable them to do their jobs also provide companies with a means of rewarding and motivating. A range of cars used creatively offers a tangible, reasonably low cost means of rewarding sales performance, special responsibilities, and long and effective service. Unlike money which, too often, once spent has little to show for it, a car can be seen in the family and social group as well as by customers. There are a number of approaches:

Recognition of sales performance. In companies that have a standard fleet of cars and where there is a pronounced status or competitive need in the sales force, a top specification model can be awarded for achieving the best sales performance against target set on either a national, regional or area basis. Obviously such an award scheme can only operate fairly and effectively if all the key factors upon which performance is assessed are under the salesman's control. Because in nearly every sales force there is a compulsive prizewinner who, if he wins too often will stop others even bothering to compete, it is better to have more than one prize. Thus a top award winner might get the highest specification car in the range and two runners up would get the next highest.

This, like any other incentive, should be supplied to the winner(s) as soon as possible following the announcement, otherwise the motivational impact will be diluted.

There are advantages and obvious disadvantages in using special model cars to motivate salesmen to produce higher sales. On the plus side it works until a man wins, but when he has the best car what else is there? On the debit side there is the disappointment if he does not win again, of moving back to the standard fleet car when his prizewinning model has to be replaced.

Another complication arises if the prizewinner or runner up decides to leave the company. You are then left with a car you certainly cannot issue to the newest recruit to the sales force if you want your incentive to continue to work successfully.

Recognition of long service. Many effective, long serving salesmen become resentful when they see new salesmen getting the same model car as they have. So a different grade of car, not necessarily a larger one, can be awarded to those members of the sales force who have served a given number of years. In some companies the new salesman is given a basic model; after two years' service he gets a better one and then later he has a choice of model within a price range.

Pitfalls to avoid. Because of the motivational impact a car has on sales force morale and status, great care must be taken over company car policies. Two developments in the car policies of some large companies had an extremely adverse effect on sales force motivation.

Government pay policies have led to a considerable increase in the numbers of management/executive cars provided by companies, in some cases outstripping the sales force car fleet. At the same time jobs have been regraded to enable companies to slot in more grades of personnel qualifying for cars. In more than one company, the sales force car has been downgraded to a smaller model with catastrophic consequences. Twenty-two salesmen resigned in one company and the whole policy had to be scrapped to persuade them to withdraw their resignations.

Second, companies may decide to revise the types of car for the sales force to try to redress the constant rises not only in car prices but in maintenance and running costs as fuel becomes more expensive. Again it does not necessarily follow that the sales force should end up with the smallest cars. A golden rule when revising car policies and schemes is never to allow the company accountant to have the final say. If he has never been a salesman, and very few have, he will tend to regard a car as a cost item capable of being pruned and ignore the human implications which can be far more important. It only needs one salesman to leave and for the company to have to incur all the expense of replacing him for every penny of that paper-saving to be wiped out.

The following verbatim comments, taken from the Management Survey Report *Business Cars* [1] covering the year to beginning of February 1976, summarise reasons for making no changes to downgrade cars at the expense of the sales force:

> If you downgrade, you've got to downgrade starting at the top level. This is all very well if you can get managers to accept it, but what do you do with the basic grade salesman who needs the car he's got now to do his job?
>
> His sales can be seriously affected by turning up in a cheaper car. I'd rather control my running costs tightly and not risk all the trouble of convincing the men that it's in the company's interests to change down. You can't guarantee that they will believe it and they don't think the neighbours will believe the reason either when they're seen running a smaller car.
>
> When management makes a conscious decision to change to less expensive types of car, it should evaluate this against the dissent it can create in unsettling managers. In many cases the vehicle is a status symbol not only in the business world but in the drive at home. We know of managers who would forego a salary increase before having the type of car reduced in standard. A decision to downgrade (cars) can have a major effect on the company's internal and external relationships.

This last reference is to managers. Let me give an example which presents the problem in even clearer form for the sales force and underlines the danger of approaching solutions from what appears to be a logical and at the same time attractive base. A national company selling food products through wholesalers employed a small sales force of eight. These men had historically been given the largest Ford range of cars because of the mileages they clocked up each year - on average about 50,000. When the company became part of a larger group, inter-company evaluations were carried out in an attempt to grade jobs so as to facilitate ease of transfer and promotions. These eight salesmen, when their jobs and benefits were examined, were deemed to have a higher grade of car than was appropriate. It was decided by the senior management that these salesmen should be given a smaller grade of car and to soften their reaction to this each man would receive a salary increase of £200 a year. The cars were purchased and the salesmen were requested to attend a sales meeting at a hotel to be told of the change in car policy and to hand over their present car and collect their new one. As soon as the announcement was made by the sales director, eight salesmen without collusion or discussion wrote out their resignations. Faced with this massed opposition, the sales director climbed down and the salesmen kept their original cars.

Such far-reaching policy decisions should never be made without prior consultation with those who will be most affected by it. Incredible as it may seem in this case and it is far from being an isolated one, no one thought to ask the salesmen what their attitude to such a change in car policy might be.

3 Further education

Younger, better educated salesmen and saleswomen are being recruited every year by companies and better initial product and sales training is being introduced and given to new entrants compared with that given to their more experienced colleagues.

Too often these older salesmen are neglected and their rusty or total lack of knowledge of current practice threatens both their security and their status and dignity, particularly when it is exposed in public at group training sessions.

Ensure therefore that your older salesmen get the necessary training to keep them up to date. But do not expose them by putting them one at a time on a course with a new intake. Better to take a group of older men together, or if yours is a very small company and this is impractical, send them on proven external courses.

4 Family recognition

Genuine thanks for good work expressed in a greetings telegram or personal letter to individual salesmen can do wonders to boost morale and motivation. Some sales managers even keep salesmen's birthday dates as well as those of their families and mark such anniversaries with greeting cards. Others express thanks to salesmen's wives by sending flowers or taking both the man and his wife out to dinner once a year. All such acts, provided they are inspired by sincerity and do not offend, will help to communicate your respect for the worthwhile job a salesman is doing and the contribution he and his family are making to the company's prosperity.

6.2 Conclusion

The dignity and status of every member of your sales force is important and must be respected. The degree and importance attached to status will vary from one person to another. Generally, as salesmen get older they can become quite touchy about their perceived status in the company hierarchy, particularly if younger men have overtaken them and been promoted into management. Try always to forecast the status implications of any decisions you are planning to implement *before* you act. At one extreme you may have to sack one or more salesmen. But at the other extreme it may be the way you conduct a sales meeting. To remember at the outset to ask the most senior member of the sales force for his opinion first before anyone else is invited to express their views may not sound all that important to you. But if it makes him feel important, if it helps him to feel that he matters, if he goes home and says to the family 'it was a good meeting - I spoke', if doing it has helped that man's status then it has been worthwhile. Always ask yourself before you act or speak what the effect is likely to be on the individual. Be sure that your management colleagues in other departments who communicate with the sales force abide by the same principle. The chairman of a company was asked to say a few appropriate words of encouragement to the sales force at the start of their annual conference. He spoke in glowing phrases of their fine work, saying that sales and profits were up. He then ended: 'Our great company is only great because of our sales force. Without you we are nothing. So thank you all for doing a great job.' Immediately following his talk a coffee break was announced. The chairman went to the cloakroom with a boardroom colleague and passed the remark, 'You know Harry, every time I see that vast sales force of ours and think what it costs I ask myself couldn't we find a cheaper means of selling our products?' Then a lavatory chain pulled and from a cubicle emerged one of the chairman's 'great sales force.' You can imagine with what security, peace of mind and wellbeing he returned to the conference after overhearing those few words.

Note

[1] Management Survey Report No. 32, *Business Cars*, British Institute of Management, 1976.

7 The need for job satisfaction

In nearly every study of human behaviour, the need to find job satisfaction has been identified as a major motivator. Maslow described it as 'self-actualisation' and McGregor implied it in his Theory Y concept. Herzberg listed several needs under the heading of satisfiers or motivators which provide a useful framework for sales managers formulating a motivational policy and approach. They include:

1 The work itself
2 The need for recognition
3 The need to achieve
4 The need for advancement
5 The need for personal responsibility and growth

Two factors are common to them all: first, they are intrinsic to the job itself and second, they are, to a very large extent, capable of being satisfied through the development of *knowledge*, job *skills* and *expertise*.

Because Herzberg has been such a persuasive advocate of his theories, there is a danger in making the general assumption that all you have to do is to 'enrich' the sales job in all these five main aspects on a blanket basis and everyone's need for job satisfaction will be met. *You do not automatically produce a strongly motivated group of people by such a blunderbuss approach.*

Job satisfaction means different things to different people. Here, as in every other area of human need, *a satisfied need is not a motivator of human behaviour.* Failure to recognise this fact has been one of the root causes of many unsuccessful programmes of job enrichment.

The pharmaceutical industry offers a very vivid example of this problem. Traditionally, selling is seen as the art and skill of persuading someone who, at the outset of a sales interview, is reluctant to buy that he should do so. To achieve this objective, the salesman uses a repertoire of techniques to raise the prospective customer's perception of the need to buy to a point where he acts upon that need. On the salesman's part the need to *win* is invariably high and an order is the essential evidence of conquest and victory.

No such tangible evidence of success is possible for the salesman or saleswoman selling prescription medicines to doctors. The doctor can promise to use a drug but it may be months before he sees a patient with a complaint for which that particular drug is the best treatment.

In 1966 one company which had been supplying compounds to other manufacturers decided to market and promote its own branded drugs. An initial sales force was recruited by the well known means of offering high salaries to attract good quality salesmen from competitors. The force that came together was an unusually competitive group of people. Commission and bonus schemes were tried and for the reasons already given in Chapter 3, these failed to motivate. The senior management, with more enthusiasm than enlightenment, then decided to go fishing in the behavioural scientists' ponds for any new means of satisfying the unquenched appetites of these highly competitive salesmen. Involving the salesmen in target setting was introduced and among other measures Edward de Bono was asked to stimulate ideas with his 'lateral thinking.' All this was to no avail because their basic need to compete and to win was not being satisfied. Today no member of that initially recruited group remains in the company. They have all found elsewhere their individual race tracks upon which they can in more tangible and measurable form satisfy their competitive instincts.

Nevertheless, on an objective basis I am going to draw on Herzberg's motivating factors in the following examination of the need for job satisfaction. Furthermore, the time, money and training you invest in all or any one of these factors will be cumulative and additive in its effect and longer lasting than any actions you take to correct or reduce sources of dissatisfaction.

These are the areas to which you should direct your time, research and efforts once you have ensured that *remuneration* and *direct incentives, security* and *status* factors are not operating as *disincentives*. The removal of causes of dissatisfaction, while not in itself likely to be motivational, nevertheless creates a climate in which, by developing the positive aspects of the sales job, more enduring motivation and job satisfaction can be achieved.

Before we examine what you can do, we need to define job satisfaction. This has become an umbrella term under which it is all too easy to start making rather glib general assumptions. Remember that every man and woman is an individual with his or her own unique pattern of needs to be satisfied, fears to be stilled and personal aspirations to be fulfilled.

Job satisfaction describes the extent to which an individual's needs are met in the day-to-day performance of his job.

This definition does not assume that the needs of all salesmen are the same. Nor does it limit research to establish what can be done to the structure, content, challenges, interests and enjoyment of the job. For one man job satisfaction may mean: 'I want to stay a salesman because I enjoy seeing the tangible results of my work at first hand and would not do so if I went into training or management. But I want my work to be fulfilling and perhaps creative, not just repetitive and boring.' For another it could mean just the opposite: 'I am prepared to learn how to sell and prove that I can, but what I really enjoy and find satisfying is organising others and the power this brings with it. I want the opportunity to be trained for this and the chance to find out if I can manage people.'

Now what actions can be taken to increase job satisfaction?

7.1 The sales work itself

The selling job, as we have already seen, is changing in many ways. You and your management colleagues must identify and analyse the nature and scale of these changes to ensure that the sales job in your company can be handled by one individual and has not become either impossibly broad or frustratingly narrow.

A job analysis will also indicate whether the job that *should* be performed by the salesman rather than what he is now doing calls for new knowledge and levels of skill and expertise. The following examples from three different industries illustrate the importance of identifying specific new areas of skill so that the salesmen are competent to perform their work. You cannot enjoy a job unless you can do it competently.

1 In the grocery and fast-moving goods markets a handful of buyers control something like eighty per cent of the market demand. Because of the immense financial impact of their decisions upon the profits of their companies, these buyers are becoming much more knowledgeable about *finance, negotiating* business with their suppliers and the *marketing* and *selling* implications of their purchasing decisions.

The supplying companies' sales forces who do business with these buyers perform a very different and much more complex sales job than their predecessors. Consequently such salesmen must not only be financially numerate but must also understand the financial benefits or savings which their customers will derive from each business transaction as well as the financial benefits to their own company of any concessions they make to the buyer. Likewise such salesmen must know when to negotiate and how to negotiate and when to use the persuasive art of selling. They must also understand the marketing techniques which their buyers are using. Developing knowledge and skills in these areas brings an enormous pay-off in enriching the sales jobs, in the amount of responsibility that can be delegated and in the size, scope and challenge of the resulting sales work.

2 Glass bottle and container manufacturers used to employ general salesmen who called on all existing and potential users of their products from breweries, wines and spirits companies, dairies, pickle manufacturers to pharmaceutical companies and proprietary cough medicine manufacturers. Now individual industry technology and marketing has developed to the stage where no one salesman can hope to look after such a diverse range of needs satisfactorily. As a result those markets have been identified as separate in their technology and container needs and specialist market sales forces have been created to serve, service and look after them. These salesmen and saleswomen are trained to a much greater depth in their customers' technology and markets and so are able to have a more mutually beneficial and profitable relationship. Here again the sales job has been made more challenging, interesting and rewarding yet not, paradoxically, impossibly broad. Indeed it has become much more specific in direction and in consequence more effective and more interesting.

3 The development of the British National Health Service has seen the demise of the doctor who conducts a general practice for patients from his home and the growth of group practices in which a large number of doctors work from a purpose-built centre sharing administrative and nursing facilities and in some of the larger health centres even dispensary and minor surgery facilities. In addition, doctors are continuing their medical studies after qualification at post-graduate medical centres. They are looking after more of their own patients when in hospital instead of handing them over entirely to their medical colleagues employed in hospitals. The implications of these changes on the job of the medical sales representative are far-reaching. Where once he could call and see the majority of the general practitioners in his territory say once every three months to discuss and promote his products in the context of the needs of the doctor's patients, today this is either not possible or so severely restricted as to make his job frequently intolerable.

The consequences of these developments are first, that the medical sales representative must be more knowledgeable about medicine to enjoy the respect and confidence of his professional customers so that they can rely on his information and advice; second, pharmaceutical companies are finding it easier to meet members of the medical profession at either small group meetings of six to twelve doctors or at larger gatherings in post-graduate centres. For the medical sales representative to be effective in conducting such meetings and leading or taking part in discussions, he must be trained to a high level of skill. This training is being given with the result that this type of sales job is becoming much more challenging and interesting and the medical profession is also benefiting from the salesmen's improved ability to communicate with them.

To identify these changes in knowledge, skill and expertise you need to carry out at least an annual audit of your sales force's job so that any developmental training needs can be spotted and appropriate action taken (see Table 7.1). When you have collected sufficient evidence to indicate that a job as it has existed must be restructured to enable its holder to achieve his or her sales objectives you must bear the following factors in mind:

1 When people have to learn new skills, make higher level or more complex decisions, they will tend, during the learning stage, to work more slowly and cautiously and will inevitably make mistakes. It is at this stage that first line sales management plays one of its most vital roles - being supportive and patient.

2 There is little point in developing people to shoulder more responsible sales work unless the authority needed to perform the job is delegated. Here again the attitude of first line management can either be supportive or destructive.

7.2 Contribution of sales work to company and society

When discussing status I said that everyone wants to stand 'psychologically tall' in the work, social and family groups in which he or she moves. This concept provides the essential bedrock upon which the beginnings of job satisfaction for salesmen is founded.

A salesman cannot derive any lasting satisfaction from doing a job which is not highly esteemed by his colleagues. Apart from the actions that I have already suggested, make sure that what you and other managers say about the role of the sales force is consistent, and that it is not undermined by thoughtless acts of omission or of commission.

Consider just one factor - organisation charts. Nearly every sales force is told how vital its work is to the prosperity, jobs and profits of everyone in the company. Now take out your organisation chart. Where are your salesmen shown on it? If you really believe the sales force job is as vital and important as is so often stated, then show it to be so visually.

Table 7.1
Sales job: training needs analysis

JOB DESCRIPTION	TASK	KNOWLEDGE	SKILLS	ATTITUDES	LEVEL OF EXPERTISE

7.3   Involvement in planning

Salesmen, like any group of people, want to be *consulted* and *involved* in those areas of decision making which directly affect and influence the quantity and quality of the work they do and upon which their performance is judged. They also need adequate information about factors that impinge directly upon their work in a form they can readily understand.

All the evidence about involving salesmen in planning their own work shows that provided this is carried out *before* targets are established salesmen tend to set themselves more challenging ones than management would have given them. This is partly due to the eternal optimism of some salesmen and partly wishful thinking.

But consider the positive implications of this tendency to set optimistic targets. Normally sales management would approach the target setting process with more details of the company's national policy, intentions and of some new business that may be in the offing and of other existing business that may be lost, than would be available to their salesmen. Consequently management may have to cut back a salesman's own estimate of what he thinks he can sell to a more cautious figure. A salesman who has been consulted, and then set a sales target *less* than his own estimate is much more likely to achieve it than if he had a target imposed upon him by management without any discussion or prior consultation.

Extending this principle in a controlled way, you can give your salesman as much opportunity as possible to be involved in other aspects of his work organisation such as:

1   Who should be called upon and how often
2   Call frequencies
3   Customer reporting systems, on what to report and how often
4   Complaints handling

Such involvement will commit an individual much more wholeheartedly to achieving agreed sales objectives. You will discover that 'the orders we best carry out are those we give ourselves.'

7.4   Need for information about performance

Once a salesman has set out to achieve his sales objectives he needs frequent feedback about his performance. Sales figures, new account openings, orders-to-calls ratios, and a host of other statistical information will tell him as well as you what he has achieved in terms of quantity. But like you he also needs to know where he is succeeding or failing and much more important *why*. To provide answers to these questions you need to develop an appraisal system which you and your salesmen can use to assess together those key areas of work planning, selling and sales administration which relate to the job your salesmen should be carrying out and against which you have set standards of performance which he must reach.

An appraisal system correctly designed and skilfully used will help your salesmen to overcome their difficulties and develop their skills. It is a key management tool for you to help every category of salesman to grow and achieve his individual job satisfactions as well as your management objectives.

Such a system can be used for your new salesmen at the completion of their initial field training. The completed appraisal provides you and the new salesmen with an assessment of strengths and weaknesses and shows where your subsequent training and development should be concentrated.

For all your salesmen, including the most experienced and successful, the appraisal system provides an instrument to train and develop the ambitious; to shake up the lethargic and to improve the best. The design and content of a salesman performance appraisal system are explained in detail in my book *Training Salesmen on the Job*.[1]

7.5   Need for recognition of achievements

Everyone has a need to be recognised not only for the social worth of his job but also for what he actually does. Here it is important to distinguish between actions you take to recognise the status of the selling job and recognising something a person achieves. Status we have already discussed. Recognition of personal achievement is *personal* and so needs to be done with care, taking account of the activities that warrant recognition and the person involved.

You can approach this in the following ways.

Giving recognition in front of others

When your salesmen have achieved something praiseworthy, outstanding or unusually creative, the annual sales conference or monthly sales meetings provide fitting occasions for public recognition. When you believe anyone deserves public recognition, you must give thought to *how* you are going to do it and *when*.

The following approaches are poles apart in recognising outstanding sales figures achieved by two salesmen and in their motivational impact. At one sales meeting, in the context of reviewing sales results, the sales manager casually remarked, 'By the way, the three new accounts opened by Norman helped the division to show an overall increase on last year's figures.'

At another the sales manager started the meeting as follows: 'Before we begin, just a word about the agenda. The managing director has asked me if he can join us all for lunch. He wants to thank personally two of you for some real breakthroughs you have made in opening up new business!'

For many salesmen tangible symbols of success are important. They are visible proof of achievement whereas the mention of a success at a sales conference is over in seconds and soon forgotten. Special ties, challenge shields, lapel badges, brooches and tiepins are some of the tangible awards many companies present to salesmen and saleswomen in recognition of individual achievement, of outstanding work and sustained sales performance. The enormous percentage of those who wear or display these awards is evidence of how proud they are of them.

A personal acknowledgement in print

Public recognition is one thing; confirming it in writing is equally important. A personal letter of thanks for a specific and noteworthy achievement sent to a salesman's home address can be seen by the family. It is a permanent reminder. It is not uncommon for salesmen to show such letters to their customers. Publication of achievements in the company magazine or sales bulletin is an effective way of communicating praiseworthy activities to colleagues in the working group. But do not debase your personal thanks by being prodigal with them. The holders of the Victoria and George Crosses awarded for outstanding acts of military and civilian valour are deservedly honoured. Those who are given titles and honours for doing their Civil Service jobs for a given number of years are not.

A salary increase

Reference has already been made to the importance of relating rewards as closely as possible in time to the effort and skill that went into earning them. Ironically, although the incentives companies try to follow this principle in the schemes devised for companies, it is still uncommon for salary increases to be awarded in the same way.

Leaving aside adjustments to salaries to keep pace with increases in cost of living, there is no reason why salary increases cannot be granted far more often than once a year. Half-yearly and even quarterly salary reviews are not only possible in some industries but can have a pronounced impact upon sales performance. There is of course the danger that when the year as a whole is reviewed a salesman's figures may not justify the award of a salary increase for figures produced in one quarter. This difficulty has been effectively catered for by a major tyre manufacturer. Half of any increase granted is treated as an addition to basic salary and the other half as a bonus. If the results are satisfactory at the completion of the financial year, then the bonus element of increases granted during the year is consolidated into salary increases.

The more a salesman can influence the way his salary moves in relation to individual effort the more salary becomes a motivator rather than a source of dissatisfaction. As one salesman who worked for a firm where salaries are reviewed quarterly put it: 'it is not just the extra money that matters, those increases act as a personal barometer of my performance and that is important to me.'

7.6 Need to achieve

The need to achieve success is as fundamental in the sales job as in any other occupation. Salesmen want to see a job completed, to solve problems and to see the tangible results of their work. Selling is a dynamic activity in which to achieve new sales targets, open up new markets, or introduce a new product or process enlarge an existing customer's business. You can help your sales team collectively and individually to achieve these things more thoroughly, more creatively and more often. The sales job is often regarded by those who do it as a journey round the same patch week in week out. Calling on the same people can become monotonous. It need not be. Of course there will be a percentage of routine calls that have to be made but you can set *specific* and challenging goals for each salesman to develop new business and take part in a programme to help achieve them.

'Brainstorming' problem prospects

In every sales territory there are usually two or three worthwhile prospects whom for one reason or another the territory salesman has not succeeded in converting into customers. Converting such worthwhile prospects can often be speeded up by small teams of salesmen holding 'brainstorming' sessions to discover new approaches, better answers to objections etc. Brainstorming is a creative technique by means of which a group of people generate a large number of ideas in a short time.

A cosmetics and soap manufacturer held a series of weekend 'brainstorming' sessions in small groups made up of the area manager, his six salesmen and an outside expert as chairman. A major prospect in each salesman's territory was brainstormed on the following basis.

First, each salesman gave his colleagues a factual background of the prospect, e.g. name; contacts; type of customer; size of business; the competitor currently holding business. Then he described the calls he had made on the prospect; the objectives he had set for each call(s); who he had met; how he opened each sales interview and the reactions; how he had presented his case; the objections raised and how he had handled them; how he had tried to close the calls and the answers he had received to his requests for the business. The pertinent details were written up on a blackboard to make recall easier.

Second, armed with this knowledge about the prospect, the chairman then invited the team to think about each of the following aspects: the amount of information known about the prospect; the alternative methods of approaching the prospect to those so far used; developing a new creative strategy and approach for this prospect. Throughout these discussions four guidelines were borne in mind:

1   *Judgement was suspended* and all ideas were considered without criticism.
2   *Everyone could freewheel* - the wilder the ideas the better. After all, none of the ideas so far attempted had produced results.
3   *Quantity* - the more ideas generated the better.
4   *Cross fertilise* - one idea helped to combine and improve the ideas of others.

At the conclusion of the freewheeling discussion during which ideas and approaches were recorded on blackboards, the chairman then drew together those that could be used to develop a customer strategy. A number of lessons were learned from these sessions of which the following were the two most notable. Incidentally in one area four of the six customer strategies that were developed produced new business.

Lack of relevant customer information. Salesmen had insufficient knowledge of the customer's needs, market situation and business problems such as his costs and profit margins. Lacking this, the salesmen made 'sales pitches', talking about their products and pushing what they had to sell but not relating to the customer. The customers, feeling under pressure and unable to see their needs reflected in the salesman's presentations, refused to buy.

*Trying to achieve too much too quickly.*Salesmen saw each sales call as self-contained instead of part of a number of calls forming a coherent strategy which would ultimately lead to success based upon a series of progressively achieved objectives. This one-shot approach had led to salesmen regarding each call as a win or lose situation. The objectives set for such *ad hoc* approaches were either wrong or over-ambitious.

Changing sales territories

However dedicated and hardworking they are, salesmen of all ages will find that their aim to achieve one hundred per cent sales success with every customer is an ambition they will never realise. There is in every human relationship what Robert Townsend has called 'the chemistry of vibrations'. In our social and business lives there are some people with whom we feel an instant rapport and compatibility; with some a neutral feeling; whilst with others for no apparent reason we feel an almost instinctive hostility. Salesman-customer relationships are no different. There are some buyers who will never buy from a particular salesman however good his product or service whereas they would buy the same product if sold by another man with whom they felt compatible. Surprisingly little is known about this human chemistry.

Nevertheless experiments in moving salesmen from one sales territory to another, if only for a short period, say three months, have produced some notable additional business without any loss of existing customers.

In one very remarkable experiment in which I took part the results were dramatic. A company in the motor and allied trades decided to secure key distributors through whom it sold its products on long term exclusive contracts the terms of which were very attractive.

Over a period of the year which had been decided as the time for securing specific distributors the majority had been signed up but in every sales territory a handful of distributors refused to do so. Reviewing the deal offered the company came to the conclusion that since there was no logical explanation for their refusals it must be the salesmen selling the deal who were the cause of the problem.

So every salesman throughout the UK was moved to a new sales territory for three sales periods totalling thirteen weeks and set the specific sales objective of signing up the few distributors the company wished to obtain. At the end of this campaign ninety-one per cent of the remaining distributors had been secured on contract.

7.7 Need for advancement

Not everyone wants advancement or the responsibilities of management but those who do should be made aware of what opportunities there are, the qualifications needed and above all that there are training facilities to develop and test management skills.

Growing your own management has always been regarded as a luxury only large companies can indulge in or afford. It is not true. Small companies are far more vulnerable than large ones if they do not. When a company starts out in business with a good idea, product or process its first priority is to sell sufficient volume to cover its costs. The entrepreneur at this stage in the life cycle of his company recruits a sales force of maybe one or two people who he hopes can and will sell successfully. He rarely thinks about the *management* potential of his first recruits. If business grows and he needs to enlarge his sales force he then appoints a sales manager. He usually makes his choice from his existing sales force. Whether the person chosen succeeds will more often than not be a matter of chance rather than design because when recruiting his first team of salesmen and saleswomen he did not deliberately decide to include one or more with management potential. Or if he did the pressure of work has denied him the time and opportunity to test and assess this potential managerial talent. The consequences of this all too familiar pattern are predictable.

If his first sales management appointment fails disastrously, either the entrepreneur's business fails or he sacks the sales manager and finds a replacement. The replacement is frequently brought in from outside. The morale of the sales force, lowered by a colleague's failure, is not raised by this decision. The very opposite happens since one or more will probably have felt that he should have been given the chance to prove he could do the job rather than an outsider who does not know the business and who has not done the pioneering work that created the job anyway.

If you have in your sales force individuals who really want to advance and manage others, then unless you can satisfy that need, they will leave.

Here let us make an assumption - but one backed up by plenty of historic evidence. Companies are rather like individuals. They tend to be 'perpetually wanting' organisations. Their owners and directing executives want initially to survive and then to grow. To grow successfully requires the presence of a sufficient pool of human talent that can assist growth and manage the business.

How can you assess those in your sales force who have management potential in a practical way?

First let us state what in overall terms a sales manager's objective is and then identify the key tasks he has to carry out to achieve that objective. A sales manager is responsible for achieving planned sales objectives *through* the efforts of his sales force not for it. To do this the sales manager must carry out five key tasks:

1   Set specific sales objectives
2   Plan the sales operations
3   Recruit and select a sales force
4   Train and develop the sales force
5   Motivate and control the sales force

The manner in which one individual carries out those tasks and the quality of results produced distinguishes one manager from another, good from bad. Style of leadership, the ability to analyse problems, reach decisions and implement them are all inseparable elements of the management job.

But as a start you can systematically involve each one of your salesmen in some of these five key tasks of the management job, setting standards beforehand so that you can build up a bank of knowledge which will help you to identify future management.

The criteria upon which you set training objectives for these five tasks are that they should describe:

1   What the trainee should be able to do at the end of the training.
2   The conditions under which he should be able to do it.
3   The standards of performance he should be able to achieve.

Sales force involvement in every aspect of management is not always practical or even desirable, for example in planning sales operations, recruitment, selection and motivation. But there is one key task in which all salesmen can be developed and that is the collective and on-the-job sales training of the sales force.

Whatever else a manager does well his ability to achieve planned results through others will hinge upon whether he can train and develop people or not. *If he cannot train he cannot manage anyone.*

Here then is one of the most effective ways in which you can implement a development programme to assess your salesmen's management potential - training them to train other salesmen.

The pay-off is twofold. Salesmen who have been trained to train others invariably improve their own selling skills. Second, salesmen trained in this way provide the sales manager with an additional development resource when he recruits more than one salesman and needs help with initial field training. And above all the training enables the sales manager to assess a salesman's capabilities in a vital area of the management job without first having to promote him into a management position.

7.8 Need for personal growth and responsibility

The great majority of salesmen, whilst not seeking management jobs, nevertheless do want to advance in terms of responsibility within the work they do. The Chinese found out years ago that in any group of a hundred prisoners there are not more than 10-15 leaders. Using this knowledge to deploy their soldiers economically they would lock up the natural leaders. They were able then to reduce dramatically the numbers of soldiers needed to guard the remainder because without a leader they lacked the initiative to escape. A study carried out in the UK in 1964 confirmed the existence of a similar percentage of leaders among British workers.

Over the last fifteen years I have put to countless hundreds of groups of sales managers this question: 'If you could keep the salary you earn now, the perks that go with your management job such as first class rail travel, higher status car, etc. and you could choose either to stay in your management job or go back to selling what choice would you make?' Eight out of every ten managers have said they would go back to selling! Exploring the reasons behind their answers I discovered, not surprisingly, that whilst all salesmen want the status symbols that go with management very few really want or enjoy the management job when, too late, they find out what it entails.

What do the majority of salesmen want? They want training initially to equip them to do their selling job effectively and successfully. Then as they mature they seek the goal of perhaps wider, more interesting and in some cases more responsible selling, training or other activity and recognition of this work in status and financial reward. Indeed you could say that he seeks to achieve by these means the status symbols that go with management - and why not? In every company we need to have many ladders up which people can climb to reach their own personal goals of job satisfaction and self-fulfilment.

It is an indictment of many companies that they have offered tinsel to salesmen in the shape of grand sounding titles, in some instances bigger cars but not *real* enlarged selling responsibilities to match their technical capabilities. As universities, technical colleges and other centres of education produce a more educated society, the extent to which selling as a job will continue to attract candidates and appeal as a career will be the degree to which it meets their interests and developing expectations.

Training and developing competent salesmen to shoulder more responsible sales work rewards the individual, the customer and not least the company.

Obviously there is no point in giving a salesman the opportunity to move into sales training, key accounts selling or product management unless he or she is given the training to perform a new job competently. But once that training is available the number of ways for people to 'grow' can, as Figure 7.1 shows, be dramatically increased. The salary grades, cars and status packages would be equal for all jobs on the same level. See Figure 3.1.

The model shown in Figure 7.1 would be relevant to a manufacturing company employing a 50-100 sales force with a sales training function, senior salesmen to develop key major accounts and product and marketing organisation.

Now let us consider an industrial company selling valves with a total sales force of twenty including the sales manager and two field sales managers. This particular organisation found that with very limited management opportunities it had to do something to maintain a stable,

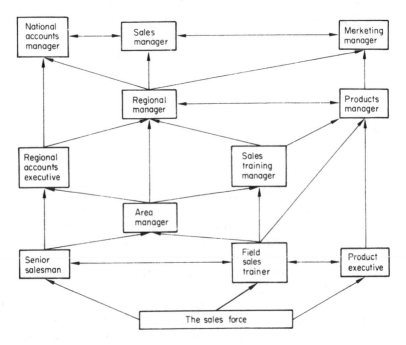

Fig. 7.1 Ladders of growth (fast-moving consumer goods company)

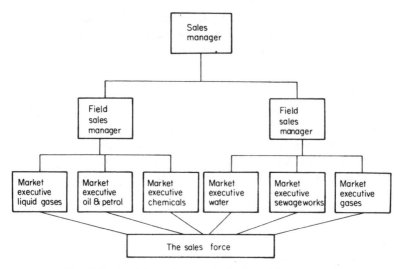

Fig. 7.2 Ladders of growth (industrial company)

productive and motivated sales force. At the same time any change that increased sales force costs could only be justified if the end result was a marked increase in business.

An analysis of the company's markets revealed that it had at least six highly profitable markets each with distinct and in some cases complex technologies, e.g. North Sea gas, oil, petrol, liquid chemicals, water, sewage works' liquid oxygen. Historically the company had split the country into geographically balanced sales territories and appointed salesmen to each one who then sold the valves to all end users.

The company decided to retain a small general sales force to sell its products to a defined list of customers and to create market managers to develop business in specific markets such as gas, oil, chemicals etc. These market managers, trained in greater depth and in how to develop major customer strategies, were given increased salaries, different cars and a much wider job which included overseas travel where appropriate. This move, initially costly, resulted in greatly increased business over a three-year period and of course opened up much wider job opportunities and prospects for the whole sales force. The revised structure is shown in Figure 7.2.

7.9 Conclusion

Meeting your salesmen's individual needs for job satisfaction is probably one of your most challenging sales management tasks. It is also a rewarding one. But once again be warned against the danger of assuming that job satisfaction means the same thing to everyone. All the evidence disproves this generalisation. What I have tried to do in this chapter is to provide some answers to the fundamental question: *How can selling be made a creative and progressive job in itself wherein an individual can grow and be rewarded in terms that compare favourably with those accorded to people who go into management?*

If you fail, then one of two things will happen; either salesmen you want to keep will leave and all your investment in their development will be lost, or they will stay and go into psychological semi-retirement on full pay.

Note

[1]   John Lidstone, *Training Salesmen on the Job* (2nd Edition) Gower Press, 1986.

8 How to identify motivational needs

When a new sales manager is appointed, in the great majority of commercial, industrial and service companies he inherits an established sales force recruited by one or more of his predecessors. It is the exception rather than the rule for him to be able to pick a completely new team. This normally only happens when a new company starts operating or a new sales division of an established firm is created.

The motivational implications of taking over an existing sales force are considerable:

1   If the sales manager is new to the company, then he has the challenging job of getting planned profit and sales targets achieved through a group of people of whose individual needs and motivations he has only the most superficial impressions.

2   Even if he has been promoted from the ranks of the sales force, he will only know individual members of the team as colleagues, as rivals and perhaps one or two as friends. He is unlikely to have reflected deeply or diagnostically upon their needs and motives in life.

3   In either case, the new sales manager brings to the job his own *personal standards*, his own *needs and motivations* to be satisfied and his own *tolerances* and *prejudices* about those who now work for him.

4   He will be temperamentally most comfortable with those subordinates who are like him or at least not superior to him in technical competence; strength of character; education and general level of cultural achievement; and intelligence.

5   He will prefer a team of salesmen who subscribe to the same moral and ethical values and standards as he does and who come from similar socio-economic backgrounds. People from different cultural and social backgrounds tend to produce the almost instinctive reaction expressed in the caption to a famous Punch cartoon of 1854:
    Who's 'im, Bill?
    A stranger!
    'Eave 'arf a brick at 'im.

6   At the outset of his managerial career a sales manager prefers a

sales force in which there are no immediate or serious threats to his security.

7   Nor does it necessarily follow that his tolerance for competition increases as he continues in the job unless he is very ambitious for the next move and has been told he will not be promoted unless and until he both *identifies* and *develops* a competent successor.

These seven factors influence the way in which a sales manager leads, communicates with, motivates and controls his sales force and how successful he will be.

The sales manager's own standards, expectations and tolerance of competition will create the climate in which the sales force he inherits works. Inevitably this climate, pleasing to some and intolerable to others, will determine:

1   Which kind of salesmen in terms of personality and qualifications can work successfully for him and can be regarded by him as performing satisfactorily.

2   Those salesmen who are compatible with the sales manager and in consequence are likely to stay, be productive and be motivated by him.

3   Those salesmen not bad enough to sack and not good enough to keep, who will remain only as unco-operative troublemakers - the candidates for the counselling couch.

4   Those salesmen who are totally incompatible, where the only solution is their departure either voluntarily or by request.

For these reasons changes in sales management frequently lead to changes in sales force personnel: 'the new broom sweeps clean'. Any new manager will either consciously or unconsciously want to build a team that will be *stable, productive,* meet his personal expectations and above all will be *motivated* by him.

If this manager is then replaced or promoted it is quite possible that his successor may have diametrically opposed personal standards, expectations, likes and dislikes. As the chemistry of vibrations begins to take effect on his team the pattern of events just described repeats itself.

The success of these salesmen under their new sales manager is less a function of their real competence than of the *pure chance* whether their faces fit and please him. This same phenomenon occurs when a salesman is transferred from one manager to another.

The success of most productive sales forces has its origins in the congruent relationship between the sales manager and his team. Yet in most instances stable, productive, motivated and well led sales forces evolve by trial and error, rarely by design. A compatible one develops by chance.

Such human upheavals as I have described and frequently witnessed are not only uneconomic but in human terms involve very painful process:

1 Long serving, loyal and competent salesmen are lost to the company.
2 Such salesmen are often replaced by less competent people who conform to the new sales manager's standards and expectations. Sometimes they are recruited from his previous company, providing him with the security of a friendly face and support while he establishes himself.
3 This game of commercial musical chairs disrupts morale, lowers productivity and efficiency and has helped to swell the ranks of white collar trades union membership.

The factors listed indicate the need to develop a practical system which sales managers can use to identify patterns of human behaviour and individual motivations and that will help them to build and maintain a cohesive, compatible, successful and motivated sales force. The following techniques will help you to:

1 Identify the motivations your sales jobs can satisfy
2 Identify the motivations of candidates who have applied to join your sales force
3 Identify the morale and motivation of your sales force

The two techniques are a systematic approach to recruitment and selection; and employee opinion polling.

8.1 Systematic approach to recruitment and selection of sales personnel

Mistakes made in the selection of salesmen due to the lack of any systematic approach are legion. Every company can and should develop a system and train sales managers in its use.[1]

When you plan to recruit a new salesman to fill a vacancy in your sales force you need two vital pieces of information to help you in your search and selection:

1 A *job description* to answer the question: 'What is the sales job I want done?'
2 An *employee profile* to answer the question: 'What kind of person will be required to do this job successfully?'

These two documents provide the cornerstones upon which all effective and successful recruitment and selection campaigns are founded. Here I propose to examine the motivational factors listed in the employee profile only.

To make this profile as accurate as possible you should construct it under specific factor headings. These factors reflect the answers to two questions upon which you must always satisfy yourself before a candidate is acceptable for the job. Just as important, it will help him to assess whether the job will meet his needs and aspirations:

1 What *can* he do? - by reason of his measurable qualifications and experience.
2 What *will* he do? - by reason of his particular character, job motivations and interests and maturity.

These 'can do' and 'will do' factors you ignore at the risk of recruiting marginal people. No matter how well qualified an individual may be, unless he 'can do' the job by reason of all the factors you have set down as essential, and 'will do' the job by reasons of his *motivations* towards the sales job in your company, you should reject him. An employee profile format which has been found most suited to the recruitment and selection of salesmen and saleswomen is shown in Table 8.1.

One of the most important parts of this employee profile and one of the most difficult to construct is identifying the *individual motivations* your sales job will satisfy. Here you are concerned with analysing and writing down under specific headings what your sales job has to offer to satisfy the needs of the type of candidate you want to attract to fill the position. Your task at the interview stage will then be to assess the candidates' individual needs and motivations and the extent to which they match the profile of what you can offer.

Let us analyse the principal job motivations which will include the five listed in Chapter 1.

Money

Does the job you wish to fill offer the salesman high earning opportunities based upon individual effort in commission, or is it paid by straight salary with little chance to earn much in bonuses or commission? How does the money you offer compare with similar sales jobs in other companies or competitors? One international food and confectionery manufacturing group pays the highest salaries in the industry to the extent that the best people cannot afford to leave. Many want to join them, though.

Table 8.1
Employee profile format

Factors	Essential	Preferred	Negative
'Can do' factors			
1 **Appearance and impact**			
2 **Measurable factors**			
Age			
Sex			
Experience			
Education (including professional qualifications)			
Special qualifications			
Intelligence			
Availability			
Driving licence			
Health			
'Will do' factors			
3 **Character traits** - need for			
Stability (maintaining same job and interests)			
Industry - willingness to work			
Perseverance - finishing what he starts			
Ability to get along with others			
Loyalty			
Self-reliance			
Leadership			
4 **Job motivations** (not already satisfied off the job) - need for			
Money			
Security			
Status			
Power			
Perfection			
To compete (competitiveness)			
To serve (service)			

Factors	Essential	Preferred	Negative

For job satisfaction:
  work itself
  recognition
  to achieve
  for advancement
  for personal responsibility and
    growth			

5 **Degree of emotional maturity** Dependence Disregard of consequences Incapacity for self-discipline Selfishness Exhibitionism Pleasure-mindedness Unwillingness to accept responsibility			

Direct incentives

These cover all the many and varied systems of payment in kind made to salesmen for achieving specific short term sales objectives. These include merchandise awards, points schemes, holiday incentives and 'salesman of the year' prizes. If you operate such direct incentive schemes, have you analysed the type of salesmen they help to motivate in your existing sales force and are they the type you want more of? If yes, then write this into your profile under direct incentives.

Security

Salesmen have a far more deep seated need for security than most sales managers realise. By the very nature of the work he does, the salesman has socially one of the loneliest jobs in commerce. And, since he is employed to persuade customers to buy from him and not all will do so, he cannot avoid being rejected quite frequently. This rejection of his products he often sees as a rejection of himself and this fuels his feelings of insecurity. You should frankly answer the question therefore: how much *security* does a sales job with your company offer? Are you a womb-to-tomb organisation offering a long term secure opportunity as is the policy of many Japanese, German, Dutch and Swiss companies? Or do you deliberately practise a policy of planned insecurity?

Do you provide clear goals and agreed standards so that salesmen know what constitutes a satisfactory level of performance? This is a particularly important form of security for candidates considering 'missionary' selling jobs such as pharmaceuticals, brewing, promoting to specifiers such as architects, where no orders are taken and it is difficult to know on a day-to-day basis if one has been successful or not.

Do you provide the security of frequent and strong supportive leadership in the field for your salesmen?

Status

Because of the nature of their job and not least the attitude that many people still have about selling, salesmen's needs for status is probably the most difficult to gauge or to comprehend. The problem is compounded by you as a manager if you use your own status needs as guidelines in analysing those your sales job can satisfy for the people you want to attract. It is often better to obtain the advice of an outsider who can assess objectively what status needs your job satisfies for the most effective of your existing salesmen.

The following questions to which you should find answers will help you to complete this section of the employee profile:

1   Is your company considered a leader in its particular field and one that salesmen would be proud to work for?
2   Is your company highly respected by customers and competitors?
3   Do you sell high quality products?
4   Will the sales job with your company bring the job holder into contact with senior or influential people? One salesman is frequently the centre of attentive and admiring audiences. He works for a games manufacturer. That is not the status factor but the type of customer to whom he sells many of his products is: he is the national accounts executive responsible among other things for sales of 'special lines' to stately homes. 'When I was lunching with the Duke of *x*' is a good opener for a conversation, isn't it?
5   Do you provide a status type car? One shirt manufacturer at the start of its UK operations recruited four salesmen to pioneer sales through retail gentlemen's outfitters. It supplied these four salesmen with chauffeur-driven Austin Princess limousines. You can imagine the status this gave them in their neighbour-

hood and not least in the eyes of their customers as the chauffeurs preceded the salesmen into the shop carrying their trade samples.

6   Do you give your salesmen status titles? Be careful of this one. The title must be respected.

Power

Here you are analysing the extent to which your salesmen have any delegated power to command or control either people or policies. Selling does not normally offer much opportunity to satisfy the need for power. You should cross refer to your profile notes under leadership requirements. If you are seeking leadership in your candidates then the man or woman appointed may be delegated powers in relation to the job - e.g. if you are analysing the powers of a national accounts executive responsible for negotiating deals worth hundreds of thousands of pounds with multiple chains, supermarket groups, then he will have considerable latitude.

Perfection

Because perfection and shortage of time characteristic of most sales work don't go together, sales jobs do not often satisfy the needs of the perfectionist. Indeed, if you have an extremist in this area of need in your sales force, he can be costly through taking twice as long to complete his work as others do. What he does may be faultless but he does not do enough of it to pay for himself and make a profit contribution. Having said that, there are sales jobs where the satisfaction of this need in moderation can be helpful. The following questions will establish whether your sales job falls within this category:

1   Do you sell products where it is *essential* for the salesman to be meticulous in explaining usage, dangers and drugs to doctors; selling dangerous chemicals to industry; demonstrating fire prevention equipment; selling to specifiers such as architects, project engineers and scientists products or services such as precision engineering, technical equipment, computerised data, banking, technical research etc?

2   Do your salesmen have to compile outline drawings for customers for submission to your drawing office or to accompany quotations? Examples here are selling plug, ball and gate valves to, e.g. oil refineries, chemical plant; selling mobile exhibition erection services; selling laboratory equipment furniture to schools, universities, industries etc?

Competitiveness

The extent to which a sales job satisfies an individual's need to compete and win will depend upon whether you as a company foster a competitive spirit by using sales contests, publishing sales performance league tables, have 'salesman of the year awards' and similar opportunities for commercial duelling. Some companies operate in highly competitive environments which appeal to certain people; in others, among which are many of the most successful Quaker organisations, all forms of internal competition are actively discouraged. It is one of the paradoxes of those admirable companies that by all the commercial yardsticks of return on capital employed, growth and so on, they are among the leaders. Pharmaceutical companies and similar organisations where it is difficult to correlate sales results with individual effort are not the most likely companies to appeal to the competitive salesman, although some have tried with mixed reactions to introduce incentive schemes.

Service

The desire to serve is essential though it must be controlled in every salesman because they are all serving and helping others *commercially*, implying that service costs money. Beware of overstressing this factor in your analysis of needs in this section of your profile. Some people's pronounced need to serve can be an expensive luxury. Salesmen are employed to help a company make profits even if they are selling bibles. The managing director of one printer of bibles bemoaned the fact that his business attracted religious fanatics whose one desire was to use his selling opportunities to preach to customers and not sell to them. As he said 'I want good salesmen who can sell to preachers'.

Job satisfaction

1 *The work itself.* Is the sales job in your company recognised by non-sales staff to be important and respected by them?
2 *Need for recognition of achievements.* Recognition, in contrast to status, is something a salesman earns and deserves by achieving or exceeding set sales objectives. Do you as a matter of deliberate policy satisfy the salesmen's needs for such recognition by, for instance:

(a) giving named acknowledgements verbally in front of others, e.g. at sales conferences?
(b) personal thanks by letter or in customer/company news letters?
(c) token awards such as special achievement ties/badges/shields; theatre tickets, selection to go on special conventions to overseas 'glamour spots'?

(d) award of financial bonus or special salary increase?

(e) special incentive schemes?

3 *Need to achieve.* Do you have a continuous training and development policy so that salesmen can satisfy their need to achieve sales goals more thoroughly, more creatively and more often? More often than sales managers realise, salesmen leave and create an unhealthy staff turnover because they get no training or insufficient to develop their skill to overcome the problems they are continually meeting with customers. Sadly, instead of telling you this, they rationalise their decision to leave by saying they are looking for more money or promotion.

4 *Need for advancement.* Not everyone wants advancement or the responsibilities of management. But for those who do and might consider responding to your advertisements, do you:

(a) make known through appraisal interviews etc. what opportunities there are in the future?

(b) make known the qualfications/experience needed?

(c) have training facilities either internally or using external resources to develop management skills and test them?

5 *Need for personal responsibility and growth.* The great majority of salesmen want to advance in terms of responsibility within the work they do. They want training to equip them to shoulder wider selling responsibilities and for this work to be recognised in status and rewarded financially. Do you, therefore:

(a) have a policy for motivating 'career salesmen' who do not want management responsibilities?

(b) have training programmes to develop them to take specialist sales jobs such as key accounts executives, product/sales development, sales trainer?

(c) reward, as part of such a policy, those who take on these specialist sales jobs with salary increases and other fringe advantages such as different motor cars etc?

When you have constructed this employee profile you will have provided yourself with an effective means of both screening candidates who want to join your company and reviewing the motivations and other factors of individual members of your sales force.

An analysis guide to help you in your search for clues to the individual motivations of candidates is shown in Table 8.2. Some sales managers may argue that to construct such an employee profile and then be capable of identifying patterns of behaviour and motivations you have to be an amateur psychologist. The answer is that you do and most sales managers are anyway - some better than others. The art of management is being able to achieve defined objectives through other people. Unless you choose correctly the people most appropriately equipped who *can* and *will* achieve those objectives, you will fail as a manager.

So the job of a sales manager calls upon you, as it does the psychologist, to understand the 'science of the nature, functions and phenomena of people'.

8.2 Employee opinion polling

Mergers between commercial groups, company takeovers and consequent changes in management personnel are commonplace today. But such upheavals can create serious communication problems and damage the morale and motivation of employees. The promotion of a middle manager or the arrival of a new managing director on the retirement or departure of his predecessor can have equally serious repercussions for the company's work force.

The economic cost of such damage or failure to forecast the potential damage is considerable but often hidden. Nowhere is this damage to morale and motivation likely to be more pronounced or more costly in terms of reduced effort and application to the job and in lost business than in the sales force. Especially because salesmen are geographically separated from day-to-day contact with their immediate manager, let alone head office, rumour feeds upon rumour when management or policy changes are in the offing.

Even when dramatic changes are not taking place, the autocratic management style of a chief executive frequently inhibits managers from telling him the truth, particularly when it is unpalatable. It is much more comfortable - and in the short term politically less dangerous - to tell him what you think he wants to hear. Thus many senior managers become the prisoners of their position, ignorant of vital information about the true state of their companies.

In such a situation nothing will educate a new sales manager faster, let alone his directing executives, than a really accurate, penetrating poll of employee opinion. To find out what employees *actually* think about their jobs and conditions of work and pay and to learn what their beliefs and values are, a survey is needed of the entire range of opinion, surmises, prejudices of non-managerial staff. Now this is no easy task because individuals are unlikely to express their frank opinions and are suspicious of any approaches to them to do so.

Many companies have used members of the personnel department to

Table 8.2

Application information analysis guide - motivations

Source of evidence	Money	Security	Status	Power	Perfection	Competitiveness	Service
Family background	Strong or weak finances at home? Attitude of parents to money. Any of own money earned?	Stable family background? Parentally? Location?	Socially conscious parents? Made to feel socially different?	Was father powerful? Did he exercise power at home?	Encouraged to perfection in manners, dress, behaviour?	Large or small family? Competed with brothers and sisters?	Encouraged to serve others? Church/scout-type activities?
Educational history	Interested in financial subjects? Earned own money whilst studying? Got qualifications in order to get more money?	Kept to same subjects because felt secure? Chose only things he knew and could do well?	Schools and colleges selected for status rather than educational achievement? Chose status courses?	Enjoyed being biggest boy or most senior because of power? Wanted to learn because of power?	Enjoyed research and detail subjects?	Enjoyed competing to be top of class or best at sport? Chose competitive situations - scholarships, awards, prizes, etc?	Worked for school? Helped others whilst at school?
Military service	Attitude to financial situation? Chose service resulting in gratuity?	Enjoyed structure? Disliked active service?	Chose status service or regiment?	Enjoyed power to command? Disliked being commanded?	Enjoyed spit and polish?	Enjoyed officer selection and training?	Enjoyed serving community? Helped others where possible?

ence	paying jobs? Paid by results? Left jobs because of money?	salaried jobs? Chose large companies? Enjoyed structure?	job with prestige companies? Enjoys status titles? Exaggerates level of job?	dominate colleagues, juniors, customers? Wants bigger job even though money similar?	work. Wants job he can do well?	competition from colleagues and other companies? Compares himself with others?	rewarding work? Wants jobs that contribute to community? Enjoys helping customers?
Outside interests	Increases earnings with part-time work? Makes money out of leisure interests?	Enjoys home-based leisure interests? Avoids dangerous sports, etc?	Chooses prestigious interests? Enjoys being council member, church warden, etc?	Enjoys power in outside interests? Sought chairman positions, captain, president, etc?	Indicates desire for perfection, e.g. model-building, rose-growing, etc?	Chooses interests where he can compete, e.g. individual sports, enters competitions and shows?	Charity work? Social or church work? Helping others, e.g. Scoutmaster, part-time teacher?
Domestic situation	Good standard of living within income? Expensive tastes?	Stable home environment? Low ambition?	He and/or wife needs social status? Climbers? Children must go to right schools?	He enjoys being boss in his own home? Attempts to decide children's future?	Spends much time improving house and garden? Wants perfect wife? Over-disciplined children?	Enjoys discussion with family and friends? Wants his children to be best at everything?	Works for family rather than himself? Encourages family in social work?
Expressed desires	Wants this job simply for pay? Willing to sacrifice to make more money? Ambition to be rich?	Wants this job because of career possibilities? Does not want to move or travel?	Wants job because of prestige? Wants to achieve social position in business?	Sees job as giving power? Enjoys power of decision over whether he takes job?	Wants to do good job in detail? Asks lots of questions about job? Detailed application form?	Wants to know who he will compete with in future? Interested in sales contests? Regards success in competitive terms?	Wants to know about customers and what they want? Sees success in terms of customer satisfaction?

carry out attitude surveys. But these have rarely revealed the truth. Personnel executives are on the company payroll. They advise and are often regarded as having considerable influence as to who is promoted, moved sideways or outside. For these reasons confidences are not easily given to them even anonymously.

To ensure that the identities of all employees taking part in the poll will be hidden and to obtain acceptance of the poll as indicating a reliable and honest desire to get at the truth, the following precautions should be taken:

1   An independent professional agency should be commissioned to conduct the poll.

2   The size and composition of the groups to be polled should be agreed.

3   The poll should be confined to employees up to the level of first line manager. Any group where there are fewer than ten people such as field sales managers should be consolidated with other small groups into a single polling unit. This will reassure such groups that their individual identities will be protected.

4   A top management executive - preferably the managing director - should personally be seen to be identified with the decision to commission the poll and to employ an outside agency to conduct it.

5   In advance of carrying out the poll, this same executive should communicate personally to all staff:

    (a)   the objectives of the poll;

    (b)   how it will be conducted;

    (c)   the total confidentiality of individual's completed questionnaires;

    (d)   that he will report back to the polled personnel *all* the findings and recommendations however critical they may be of management;

    (e)   that he will state what management proposes to do when the poll's findings and recommendations are known; and

    (f)   what management *does not* propose to do and *why not*.

6   After a simple multi-choice questionnaire has been prepared, copies should be placed in a pile and each group of employees is invited to a meeting place, selects at random the blank questionnaire he or she will complete. This provides added assurance that the forms are neither keyed nor marked in any secret way enabling a completed questionnaire to be linked to any one individual.

7   A separate series of questions should be compiled for each division, category or level of job to reflect the different technical conditions.
8   The questionnaires should be designed so that only a tick is required to answer each question. No employee should sign his name nor provide identifying marks of any kind. A sample questionnaire for polling sales personnel is shown in Table 8.4.
9   The invitation to employees to take part in the poll and to answer the questions must be on a voluntary basis.
10 Where there are supervisory levels to be polled, they should be polled first.
11 Where the staff are unionised, always advise the union in advance of your intention to conduct such a poll.
12 It does not matter when the polling is conducted with this proviso - if you do it in the employee's own time then this time should be paid for or made up in some other way.

With these precautions and assurances, 85 to 90 per cent of sales and other categories of employees will answer the questions frankly and freely. About 10 to 15 per cent will give unrealistically favourable answers, because, despite all the assurances of confidentiality they still are afraid to reveal what they honestly feel and think.

The opinion poll should be conducted in two stages.

Stage 1

Those to be polled are invited to the polling centre and meet under the chairmanship of a consultant from the independent agency. Each person completes his or her questionnaire and then places it in a ballot box.

At this meeting it is explained that the questions to be answered are probably insufficient to cover every item which might be of concern to the employees. It would be ideal to interview each person on an individual and confidential basis. However, the chairman explains:

> But this is not practical because of the numbers involved. To provide a means of communicating such additional qualitative information, we should like to talk on an individual basis to from 10 to 15 per cent of the group. We do not want management to pick this group because of the danger that those chosen may be biased. So to avoid this we should like you to indicate who among your group you feel are best qualified to present to us *accurately* and *comprehensively* a report on conditions as they exist which the questionnaire did not enable you to communicate.

Each person is then given a nomination form (see Table 8.3), and asked to *print* the names of three of their working colleagues (not from management) familiar with the group's needs and problems and to drop these forms into the ballot box with their completed questionnaires. Those nominated are tallied and used as the basis for selection of the groups' representatives for follow-up interviews.

Stage 2

Those receiving the largest number of nominations are then interviewed. But before this their names are posted to the employees so that they know to whom to communicate additional comments, information and opinions. A gap of at least two weeks should elapse between advising the groups of the names of their nominated representatives and conducting the interviews.

An interesting by-product of this polling technique is that these nominees tend to be the *natural leaders* in each group. Their feedback of information and opinions provide the most valuable and accurate insight as to *why* morale is good or bad. Furthermore they can be used as a sounding board for management's proposed changes in company

Table 8.3
NOMINATION FORM

Please give us the names of three sales representatives who are familiar with the needs and problems of your region or sales force with whom we may speak.

(Please print their first and last name)

1. ....
....

2. ....
....

3. ....
....

Table 8.4

Sample questionnaire for employee opinion poll (sales personnel)

1 The product advertising in national publications is

    (a) ___ very helpful
    (b) ___ somewhat helpful
    (c) ___ not too good
    (d) ___ almost worthless

2 Sales promotion literature sent to dealers is

    (a) ___ very helpful
    (b) ___ somewhat helpful
    (c) ___ not too good
    (d) ___ almost worthless

3 The order acknowledgement letter is

    (a) ___ very helpful
    (b) ___ somewhat helpful
    (c) ___ not too good
    (d) ___ almost worthless

4 XYZ Ltd is fair in its dealings with dealers

    (a) ___ always
    (b) ___ usually
    (c) ___ seldom
    (d) ___ never

5 The A pack, as a sales aid for use by dealers, is

    (a) ___ very helpful
    (b) ___ somewhat helpful
    (c) ___ not too good
    (d) ___ almost worthless

6 Service received in my territory on BC is

    (a) ___ very satisfactory
    (b) ___ reasonably satisfactory
    (c) ___ somewhat unsatisfactory
    (d) ___ very unsatisfactory

7   Service received in my territory on DEF is

    (a) __ very satisfactory
    (b) __ reasonably satisfactory
    (c) __ somewhat unsatisfactory
    (d) __ very unsatisfactory

8   All things considered, the GH order entry system compares with the previous IJ system

    (a) __ decidedly better
    (b) __ better
    (c) __ about the same
    (d) __ somewhat inferior
    (e) __ decidedly inferior

9   The new product and application information I receive is

    (a) __ very helpful
    (b) __ somewhat helpful
    (c) __ not too good
    (d) __ almost worthless

10   I feel that the company's handling of credit problems is

    (a) __ very satisfactory
    (b) __ reasonably satisfactory
    (c) __ somewhat unsatisfactory
    (d) __ very unsatisfactory

11   The supplies and materials (order forms, price lists, catalogue etc.) furnished me are

    (a) __ very satisfactory
    (b) __ reasonably satisfactory
    (c) __ somewhat unsatisfactory
    (d) __ very unsatisfactory

12   The sales aids (samples) and equipment the company furnishes are

    (a) __ very helpful
    (b) __ somewhat helpful
    (c) __ not too good
    (d) __ almost worthless

13 The K personnel in LMN that I work with are
    (a) __ very co-operative and agreeable to work with
    (b) __ reasonably co-operative and agreeable to work with
    (c) __ somewhat unco-operative and not too agreeable
    (d) __ very unco-operative and disagreeable

14 The order department is co-operative in processing my orders
    (a) __ always
    (b) __ usually
    (c) __ seldom
    (d) __ never

15 The service given my customers by the plant is
    (a) __ very satisfactory
    (b) __ reasonably satisfactory
    (c) __ somewhat unsatisfactory
    (d) __ very unsatisfactory

16 The plant is co-operative in getting orders shipped promptly
    (a) __ always
    (b) __ usually
    (c) __ seldom
    (d) __ never

17 I feel that dealers' complaints are handled in a
    (a) __ very satisfactory manner
    (b) __ reasonably satisfactory manner
    (c) __ somewhat unsatisfactory manner
    (d) __ very unsatisfactory manner

18 Considering my previous training and experience, the training
    given me for my present work covered
    (a) __ everything I need to know
    (b) __ nearly everything I need to know
    (c) __ only some of the things I need to know
    (d) __ very few of the things I need to know
    (e) __ I received no training

19 I receive too many bulletins from the sales department

    (a) ___ never
    (b) ___ seldom
    (c) ___ frequently
    (d) ___ always

20 Most of the reports I have to prepare are

    (a) ___ very important
    (b) ___ important
    (c) ___ rather unnecessary
    (d) ___ a waste of time

21 I am forced to handle unnecessary detail work

    (a) ___ never
    (b) ___ seldom
    (c) ___ frequently
    (d) ___ almost constantly

22 The amount of travelling I am expected to do is

    (a) ___ very reasonable
    (b) ___ reasonable
    (c) ___ somewhat unreasonable
    (d) ___ very unreasonable

23 Receiving expense and 'draw' allowances weekly is

    (a) ___ very satisfactory
    (b) ___ reasonably satisfactory
    (c) ___ somewhat unsatisfactory
    (d) ___ very unsatisfactory

24 The weekly voucher which I receive from the company is clear and
    understandable

    (a) ___ always
    (b) ___ usually
    (c) ___ seldom
    (d) ___ never

25 My job 'takes a lot out of me' physically

   (a) ___ never
   (b) ___ seldom
   (c) ___ frequently
   (d) ___ always

26 My job keeps me under considerable mental strain

   (a) ___ never
   (b) ___ seldom
   (c) ___ frequently
   (d) ___ always

27 I know what is expected of me on my job

   (a) ___ all of the time
   (b) ___ most of the time
   (c) ___ some of the time
   (d) ___ practically none of the time

28 I feel that the product lines of the company are

   (a) ___ very complete
   (b) ___ reasonably complete
   (c) ___ somewhat incomplete
   (d) ___ very incomplete

29 I feel that the company's product lines compare with competitors'
    product lines

   (a) ___ very favourably
   (b) ___ reasonably well
   (c) ___ rather poorly
   (d) ___ very poorly

30 I feel that my opportunity to advance in XYZ is

   (a) ___ excellent
   (b) ___ good
   (c) ___ fair
   (d) ___ poor

31 The over-all objectives of the company are made clear to me
    (a) ___ always
    (b) ___ frequently
    (c) ___ seldom
    (d) ___ almost never

32 I feel that company policy on price concessions is
    (a) ___ very satisfactory
    (b) ___ reasonably satisfactory
    (c) ___ somewhat unsatisfactory
    (d) ___ very unsatisfactory
    (e) ___ I don't know what it is

33 I think that XYZ salesmen have the company's best interests at heart
    (a) ___ at all times
    (b) ___ most of the time
    (c) ___ some of the time
    (d) ___ practically never

34 The field sales manager's knowledge of the problems in my territory is
    (a) ___ excellent
    (b) ___ good
    (c) ___ rather poor
    (d) ___ very poor

35 My contacts with my general sales manager are
    (a) ___ very satisfactory
    (b) ___ reasonably satisfactory
    (c) ___ somewhat unsatisfactory
    (d) ___ very unsatisfactory
    (e) ___ I have very little contact with him

36 There is friction among the salesmen in my district
    (a) ___ never
    (b) ___ seldom
    (c) ___ usually
    (d) ___ always

37 The company handles salesmen's grievances
   (a) __ in a very satisfactory manner
   (b) __ in a reasonably satisfactory manner
   (c) __ in a somewhat unsatisfactory manner
   (d) __ in a very unsatisfactory manner

38 I think that other XYZ salesmen are
   (a) __ very satisfied with their jobs
   (b) __ reasonably satisfied with their jobs
   (c) __ somewhat dissatisfied with their jobs
   (d) __ very dissatisfied with their jobs

39 I feel that the sales quotas are established on a basis that is
   (a) __ very fair and sound
   (b) __ reasonably fair and sound
   (c) __ somewhat unfair and unsound
   (d) __ very unfair and unsound

40 The number of sales contests is
   (a) __ about the right number
   (b) __ too many
   (c) __ not enough

41 Territorial adjustments made by the company have been
   (a) __ very fair
   (b) __ reasonably fair
   (c) __ somewhat unfair
   (d) __ very unfair

42 I feel that the company's method of compensating salesmen compares with other companies
   (a) __ very favourably
   (b) __ reasonably well
   (c) __ rather poorly
   (d) __ very poorly

43 I feel that the salesmen's compensation plan is
   (a) ___ very fair and sound
   (b) ___ reasonably fair and sound
   (c) ___ somewhat unfair and unsound
   (d) ___ very unfair and unsound
   (e) ___ I don't know what it is

44 I feel that the company's benefit package compares with other companies
   (a) ___ very favourably
   (b) ___ reasonably well
   (c) ___ rather poorly
   (d) ___ very poorly

45 I think that the rating of salesmen should be on
   (a) ___ personal sales only
   (b) ___ total sales (personal plus mail)

46 I think that promotions in the sales department are made on the basis of
   (a) ___ ability to do the job
   (b) ___ job ability and length of service
   (c) ___ ability, if length of service is equal
   (d) ___ length of service alone

47 The information presented at sales meetings is
   (a) ___ very helpful
   (b) ___ somewhat helpful
   (c) ___ not too good
   (d) ___ almost worthless

48 Having the sales meeting during the inactive period between Christmas and New Year is
   (a) ___ very reasonable
   (b) ___ reasonable
   (c) ___ somewhat unreasonable
   (d) ___ very unreasonable

49 In sales meetings I feel free to say exactly what I think

    (a) ___ always

    (b) ___ usually

    (c) ___ seldom

    (d) ___ never

50 The sales department keeps me informed of what is going on

    (a) ___ all of the time

    (b) ___ most of the time

    (c) ___ some of the time

    (d) ___ very seldom

51 My general sales manager keeps me informed of changes in company policy

    (a) ___ always

    (b) ___ usually

    (c) ___ seldom

    (d) ___ never

52 I am assured of help from the field sales manager in dealing with problems in the field

    (a) ___ always

    (b) ___ usually

    (c) ___ seldom

    (d) ___ never

53 My opinions are disregarded by the sales department

    (a) ___ never

    (b) ___ once in a while

    (c) ___ frequently

    (d) ___ always

54 The general sales manager and field sales manager know whether or not I am doing good work

    (a) ___ always

    (b) ___ usually

    (c) ___ seldom

    (d) ___ practically never

55 I know where I stand with my general sales manager

    (a) ___ always
    (b) ___ usually
    (c) ___ seldom
    (d) ___ never

56 I am 'bawled out' or criticised in front of others

    (a) ___ never
    (b) ___ seldom
    (c) ___ quite frequently
    (d) ___ very frequently

57 If I were to give the sales department a good suggestion in connection with my job, I am sure that I would get credit for it

    (a) ___ always
    (b) ___ usually
    (c) ___ seldom
    (d) ___ practically never

58 My efforts to improve myself are encouraged and recognised by the sales manager

    (a) ___ always
    (b) ___ usually
    (c) ___ seldom
    (d) ___ practically never

59 I think I am too loosely supervised

    (a) ___ never
    (b) ___ seldom
    (c) ___ frequently
    (d) ___ practically always

60 Certain salesmen are 'pets' and get favourable treatment

    (a) ___ never
    (b) ___ seldom
    (c) ___ usually
    (d) ___ always

61 I feel that I can count on a job with XYZ

    (a) ___ until I retire
    (b) ___ as long as I can do my work
    (c) ___ until the next depression
    (d) ___ not at all - I might lose my job at any time

62 I feel that top management is aware of the problems I am up against

    (a) ___ at all times
    (b) ___ most of the time
    (c) ___ only part of the time
    (d) ___ practically never

63 I feel that my contact with top management (other than my sales manager) is

    (a) ___ very satisfactory
    (b) ___ reasonably satisfactory
    (c) ___ not so close as it could be for me to do my best work
    (d) ___ non-existent

64 Top management is co-operating in making improvements for salesmen

    (a) ___ always
    (b) ___ usually
    (c) ___ seldom
    (d) ___ never

65 If I were offered a similar job with another company at the same or at a higher rate of pay, I would

    (a) ___ not consider changing
    (b) ___ investigate, but probably not change
    (c) ___ seriously consider it and probably change
    (d) ___ take it immediately

66 I think that chances like this to say what I think

    (a) ___ have been needed for a long time
    (b) ___ are a good idea
    (c) ___ are worth a trial
    (d) ___ are a waste of time

policy or ideas in communications. From their reactions as a group, management can decide quickly whether a proposed course of action will be consistent with the group's needs and values and be favourably received or not.

8.3 Handling employee opinion poll findings and recommendations

Having participated in such a poll, salesmen and other employees will react and be motivated or demotivated not only by what happens afterwards but how quickly it happens.

Using a computer the answers to the questionnaire can be speedily compiled, analysed and tabulated. This can be carried out while the 'natural leaders' are being interviewed. When the questionnaire findings have been assembled, consideration should then be given to editing and publishing them immediately to keep in communication with the staff on this project. A great deal of thought should be given to ensuring that this information is published in an easily understood form. Compare Table 8.5 and Figure 8.1.

The choice of *how* the information will be communicated depends upon the location of the staff to be told and will vary from the notice-board, a special news bulletin or a video-taped presentation to all staff at lunchtime in the canteen. Two factors should govern the decision to publish these findings in advance of the interview findings: first, can everyone who took part in the poll receive the information at the same time? Second, can top management state a firm date when it will not only be in a position to publish the total findings and the recommendations but, most important, what it proposed to do about them?

If these two criteria can be met then it is a good thing to provide advance information. It underlines management's continuing commitment to the purpose of the poll and moreover it keeps management in touch. All the employees will have identified the date in their minds if not in their diaries and top management will fail to deliver its promise at its peril.

When the complete report with its findings and recommendations is delivered, top management has then to face up to its implications and act.

The first hurdle to be got over is the publication of all the findings and the recommendations that have been made. The second is to tell the staff which recommendations are going to be accepted and implemented and which ones are not and why not. Interestingly and perhaps not surprisingly, the motivational pay-off from doing the latter is often

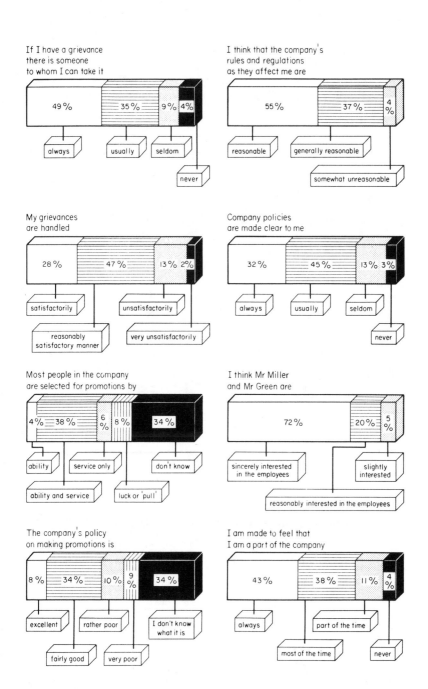

Fig. 8.1 Employee opinion poll findings - graphic presentation

Table 8.5

Employee opinion poll findings - tabular presentation

52 I am assured of help from the field sales manager in dealing with problems in the field

(a) always   (c) seldom
(b) usually   (d) never

Total Responses   15   15   13   13   14   70

	District 1 %	District 2-5 %	District 3 %	District 4 %	District 6-7 %	Total No.	%
(a)	33	67	31	46	57	33	47
(b)	33	27	46	46	36	26	37
(c)	33	-	15	8	7	9	13
(d)	-	7	8	-	-	2	3

53 My opinions are disregarded by the sales department

(a) never   (c) frequently
(b) once in a while   (d) always

(a)	27	33	54	38	29	25	36
(b)	7	53	15	23	57	22	31
(c)	60	7	31	31	7	19	27
(d)	7	-	-	8	-	2	3
No Answer		7			7	2	3

110

much more positive than people expect, but it takes courage.

In one company the poll revealed a considerable amount of incompetence at middle management level. The chief executive carried out an extensive pruning involving the departure of some people. This produced anxiety throughout the firm. But instead of trying to gloss things over the chief executive said to the staff: 'If you survive this shake up, the firm will survive and your jobs will be reasonably safe.' The survivors, knowing the ordeal was over, felt a sense of relief and buckled down to their jobs.

Note

[1]   For detailed guidelines on how to develop a proven system of recruiting and selecting successful salesmen see John Lidstone, *How to Recruit and Select Successful Salesmen*, 2nd edition, Gower.

9   Time for action

At the end of a residential training course about management and motivation, a sales manager attending it summarised his thoughts as follows: 'Now I have to leave the comfort of theory and the hygienic security of this course to return to the mess of reality.'

Theories about what influences human behaviour and motivation have been advanced and tested by thousands of experts and laymen in the past. And since mankind has an infuriating habit of confounding the experts as often as confirming their neat concepts, I have no doubt that this theorising will continue with unabated enthusiasm into the foreseeable future. But managing a sales force is a practical activity. At the heart of this job is the integral, continuing and challenging task of motivating your salesmen and saleswomen as a group and as individuals to achieve planned measurable results. The purpose of this final chapter is to indicate guidelines for action. But first let us remind ourselves of the facts of commercial life against which your motivational policies will be challenged for their relevance and tested for their realism.

9.1   Facts of commercial life

Among the many factors which now and in the next decade will increasingly influence the management and motivation of sales forces are:

1   *Continuing growth of giant organisations*
In the chapter on the salesman's need for security, I referred to the growth of companies larger in size but fewer in number. Whilst there is no compelling evidence that large organisations are more effective or more efficient than small ones, mergers and takeovers continue throughout the world, resulting in the emergence of giant organisations. Examples of this development are plain for all to see and impinge increasingly upon our daily lives from banking and insurance, brewery and building products, food manufacturing and super-marketing chains to hotels, motor car manufacturers, pharmaceuticals and shipping companies. The implications of this trend are far-reaching in terms of the nature of the types of sales jobs that emerge or remain and not least in the numbers of them.

2 *Growth of multinational companies*

A consequence of the previous factor already in evidence is the growth of multinational companies which are not only large but becoming pan European, their markets transcending national frontiers. A market or sales territory covering three or four countries has been a fact of life for many companies and their salesmen for some years. For sales managers in these situations there are a number of motivational problems to resolve including:

(a) the constant strain of travel, for example flying out from Heathrow or other European airports on a Monday morning and returning on Thursday or Friday three weeks in every four;

(b) communicating persuasively in another language and all the while observing the conventions of the country in which you are selling;

(c) minimum of frequent supportive supervision on the job;

(d) the constant disruption of family life and to the quality of life.

3 *Growing numbers of women employed in selling jobs*

As the commercial and industrial world responds to the demands, backed by law, for equal job opportunities for women and the removal of sex discrimination, more and more women are coming into selling jobs. Looking ahead, mixed sales forces are as likely to be managed by women as men.

4 *Comparatively high levels of affluence*

As more and more women decide to continue working after marriage, the joint incomes of thousands of salesmen and their wives total five figures. This brings into question the attraction of a large number of selling jobs where the prime reward and motivation offered is the opportunity to earn a lot of money. A selling job offering total earnings of say £7,500 to £12,000 a year appears to be a strong magnet to attract appropriately qualified salesmen earning perhaps £5,000 a year or less. But is it so in real terms if a man and his wife have a joint income of say £11,000 a year?

5 *Better educated people seeking interesting jobs*

A growing proportion of those who in previous generations would have started work at school leaving age, are now continuing full-time education at technical colleges and universities. At the age of twenty or twenty-one when they make their first job applications they come armed with diplomas, degrees, technical or professional qualifications.

The greater complexity of some selling jobs, particularly in areas of high technology, calls for candidates with special qualifications. There are two dangers here: one is that these academically qualified individuals may not even consider selling as a worthwhile career or alternatively they assume that the possession of a degree provides an automatic passport into a management job after a statutory but minimal period of service in the sales force. Almost inevitably an increasing percentage of members of a sales force will have higher educational qualifications but that does *not* mean they are management material and that those lacking them are not.

What this more educated potential means for company sales management is that they must find convincing answers to two questions:

(a) Can selling offer not only a satisfying and interesting job but one that is *respected* and - given proven competence by the individual - is reasonably *secure*?

(b) Can selling offer long term career prospects when there have been so many company mergers, takeovers and bankruptcies resulting in fewer jobs and redundancies at middle management level?

6 *Job security*

The governments of more and more countries are creating laws providing people with greater job security and generous social security payments when they are unemployed. Nowhere is this social legislation more apparent than in those countries comprising the EEC. Some of the consequences of these laws are already becoming apparent. Companies are becoming much more cautious in taking on additional staff because the legal implications and costs of getting rid of them when business is bad or people prove to be incompetent are so vast.

These six factors and many others are creating conditions in which the effective motivation and management of sales forces is becoming much more challenging and complicated. The personnel problems companies are having to resolve now can be traced back to lack of thought given to selection decisions made in the early 1960s and before. One of the world's largest tobacco and fast-moving consumer groups was horrified by what its personnel records revealed. Using as a data base all staff who joined the group at the start of their business careers and stayed until they retired, about 42 per cent were promoted into the top 6 per cent of management jobs including executive directorships of the main board. At first the chairman refused to believe this discovery but as management failures were identified and the reasons for them analysed he had to face the truth; insufficient thought and forecasting had been given to selection and promotion decisions. My own research in companies with similarly detailed personnel records spanning a minimum of forty years confirms these findings again and again.

9.2 A programme for action

The decisions you make and take *today* are going to have a major impact upon your company's operating costs, competitive performance and profits not just over the next twelve months but many years from now. The following questions have been set down with comments to assist in your search for answers relevant to your company. The answers will provide a basis to enable you to develop a programme of motivation to be timed and above all actioned.

1 *Do you know why men and women wish to join your company and remain?*
Assumptions are poor subsitutes for facts. You should seek answers to this question in the motives that lead people to apply to join your company, but after they become employees it is essential to validate their *real* reasons and motivations. The build-up of this bank of knowledge will enable you to become much more analytical and selective. If someone joins you for, say, financial improvement only to find that he got many benefits in kind but not in *spendable* cash, you could have a potential personnel problem that will end up either in a resignation or a dissatisfied salesman. In either case the result is expensive.

2 *Do you know why competent men and women you would like to have retained have left your company?*
When people leave, you can often learn useful if uncomfortable truths about your company so long as the person interviewing the departing salesman is not his line manager. The truth is much more likely to be revealed to someone who is trained to conduct what are often termed 'exit interviews' where the relationship with the individual has been an advisory one such as in personnel or training. The important thing to remember here is that the information obtained, if factual, usually reflects adversely upon you, or upon one or more of your present or past management colleagues. So the stature and rank of the person who collects and communicates the findings has got to be such that any changes needed can be made. For example in one company three salesmen who resigned over a period of eighteen months all gave as their main reason the lack of promotional prospects. When investigated it turned out that the sales manager at the selection interviews of each of these men had promised promotion opportunities within three years, quoting the speed of his own rapid rise in the company many years before as evidence to support this forecast.

Don't promise promotion on the basis of your own experiences. You are a manager. You are selecting others essentially to be salesmen. If there are few or no prospects then say so. If you get turned down by the ambitious then so be it. Better that than for them to join you and leave soon afterwards with all the costs, morale implications and disenchantment this brings.

3   *Do you have a systematic procedure for recruiting and selecting sales staff and have you had training to develop your skill to use this system?*

A business is made up of people. Your selection decisions are the basis not only of tomorrow's sales but next year's and the following years. So the people you pick can help to found a business; but if you pick the wrong ones the business will founder. Tell candidates the *worst* as well as the best features of a job with your company. Don't appoint overqualified candidates; it is better to appoint someone who likes the job in prospect rather than one who may be technically qualified but has doubts about the job.

4   *Has a study been made of the disincentives of the sales job?*

In far too many companies the salesman is *overchecked* and *undermanaged*. The removal of irritating disincentives can create a positive attitude to work, e.g. never introduce an additional reporting system unless you have satisfied your sales force that it is necessary and sold them its benefits. I remember reading a message scrawled across a salesman's report form just before one Christmas: 'A happy New Year to all my readers - if there are any.' There is a world of difference between managing your sales force for the results you want them to achieve and policing them.

5   *Is your remuneration system based on job grading, responsibility and objective appraisal?*

Not only this, but is the system published? If not, why not? At a public conference in London in 1971 Peter Linklater, a director of Shell UK Ltd, stated that Shell did a survey asking staff if they wanted job salary brackets and the merit rating system upon which salary adjustments were based made public. The overwhelming response was 'yes'. Further questioning revealed a widespread suspicion of the justice of a remuneration system operated in secret. If your system is not published is there any reason to suppose that your sales staff are any less suspicious about the way yours operates?

6   *Have you assessed whether your remuneration system is the most effective and appropriate to motivate your company?*

Have you ever tested your present remuneration system or compared it with the results an alternative system might produce? Probably not. Remember that a salary survey that tells you that your company is among the 'forty-six per cent paying salesmen by salary plus bonus on

116

sales target' is a meaningless piece of information. Are you going to consider testing another system? If not, why not?

7 *Do you operate a payments by results scheme?*
If your answer is 'yes' does your scheme satisfy the six essential conditions for success described in Chapter 3? If your answer is 'no' then throw it out because it won't work and isn't working now.

8 *Do you operate a sales incentives scheme?*
If the answer is 'yes' how long has it been operating without change? Remember that incentives schemes, like friendship, are in constant need of repair and maintenance. There are three rules for incentive schemes:

- (a) They need adequate maintenance to check that they are working as planned; otherwise, like cars, they will let you down.
- (b) Even well maintained schemes lose their effect with the passage of time, usually within five years of installation; salesmen and saleswomen marry; they have families; needs satisfied diminish the attraction of many money-based schemes; holiday schemes repeated year after year pall.
- (c) Because of (a) and (b) it is cheaper, easier and motivationally better to throw out your existing scheme and choose or design a new model based on the needs of the company, the needs of the customer and above all the needs of the salesmen.

9 *What ladders of job satisfaction do you provide to enable progression to be made to higher or different levels of sales responsibility?*
Remember that the fewer the ladders up which people can climb, the more the unqualified will try to climb them. The cause of many psychological breakdowns has been the result of overpromoted people. These are the people described as fulfilling the Peter Principle of having reached their first levels of incompetence.[1] For those salesmen who are not management potential, what alternative and genuine ladders of job growth and of job satisfaction can you offer them? The creation of such ladders involves more than just titles. It implies having a planned programme to develop the skills of the people who are going to occupy the positions these titles represent, e.g. train the trainer skills for field sales trainers; marketing planning knowledge and skills for product executives; finance and negotiation skills development for senior salesmen and for regional and national accounts personnel; and for those with management potential a planned programme to identify it, test and develop it. If you are not doing these things, why not?

10 *What leadership style does your sales force need and are you satisfying it?*

In Chapter 2, I described and illustrated a range of leadership styles. Questionnaires completed by sales personnel in companies all over the world asking them to list the qualities of the best managers (not the most popular, I hasten to add) they have worked for, contain many common factors. Consider Table 9.1.

Now examine your own leadership style and behaviour as a manager. Can you honestly say that you have never done any of the things listed in the right hand column? As I have already indicated leadership is a relationship between the leader and those he leads.

The choice of leadership style should be based upon three factors; first what is most appropriate for the group you manage; second what is most appropriate for each individual; and third what is most appropriate to ensure that the tasks are achieved by your team. But you must be yourself. Be natural. If you adopt a style that is a 'role', a cardboard figure totally alien to you, it will not work. What is more your sales force will probably react in one of two ways. They may say amongst themselves, 'poor old x, he has obviously just been on a course and been taught how to motivate us in ten steps but has only remembered the first three. Let's humour him for a few weeks, then he will get over it.' Or there may be deep resentment at your demonstrable manipulation of them. A salesman once said to me about his sales manager, 'The first time I met him, sincerity seemed to shine out of every word he spoke and every action he took. I was completely won over. But on the second meeting he must have forgotten to put on his motivational mask. I could see all the strings being pulled. He was nothing more than a human manipulator. From then, so far as I was concerned, I did not trust a word he spoke or an action he took.'

There are other aspects of leadership. 'How do you treat and manage women in your sales force?' is a question frequently asked by sales managers. The answer is: treat them as human beings and not as special cases. Extend to them the same respect, dignity and managerial impartiality that you give to their male colleagues - no less and no more than that. If you show prejudice against women or undue partiality, either will be resented by the women as much as by their colleagues. Another question that crops up much more nowadays is: 'how should I deal with foreigners?' Many sales managers now manage teams that contain Englishmen, Dutchmen, Germans, Frenchmen, Italians and Swedes. Again the answer is deceptively simple: treat them *not* as foreigners but as human beings with this additional proviso. Nationals of every country have their own conventions and traditions and these must always be respected. It has become popular in Britain as it has long been so in North America for sales managers and their salesmen and women to

Table 9.1
The ideal/real manager

Qualities salesmen expect from a manager:	What they too often experience: a manager who:
1 *Fairness* - does not have pets and favourites.	1 Is a 'yes-man' to his superiors.
2 *Decisiveness* - not afraid to make decisions, however unpopular.	2 Is a 'no-man' to me.
	3 Passes off the ideas of others as his own.
3 *Loyalty* - takes responsibility himself when things go wrong.	4 Stabs others in the back.
	5 Gets rid of anyone who threatens him.
4 *Expertise* - can do what he asks us to do.	6 Passes the buck when he makes mistakes.
5 *Honesty* - gives sincere praise and criticism.	7 Manipulates the facts to his own advantage.
6 *Courage* - gets rid of dead wood, tells top management the truth.	8 Blackmails me into compliance.
7 *Humanity* - treats me as a human being.	
8 *Good delegator* - shares objectives with me.	
9 *Consistency* - I know where I stand.	

speak to one another on first name terms. Such easy familiarity is not present amongst salesmen, let alone with their managers in many European countries such as France and Germany. Indeed it would be deeply disturbing to such salesmen if you tried to force, introduce or suggest a familiarity into a business relationship which they prefer to keep on a strictly formal basis.

9.3 Conclusion

It has often been said by despairing or exasperated managers that: 'it is not management that is difficult, it's people.' Yet the very essence of the management job is the ability and skill to achieve a set of planned objectives through the efforts of a group of *people* more effectively than the group could achieve as individuals if left to their own devices. But the group must want to achieve the same objectives as you do and here is the challenge. You can lead a horse to water but he will only drink if he is thirsty. You can design the most elaborate remuneration schemes, job enrichment and policies to improve job security and status. But unless they meet the needs of your sales force as a whole and the individual members of it they will not work. The behaviour of your salesmen and saleswomen and their motivations are intensely *personal* and *unique*. Yet still the majority of companies apply blanket policies to motivate their salesmen as though they had *all* come out of some identical machined moulding. Why? This may be because companies have carried out no research to discover the real profile of needs to be satisfied, which would result in people wanting to employ their full abilities in their work. Alternatively the reason may be found in the answer given by one managing director who said, 'it is administratively more convenient and less costly to treat everyone the same. We are not in business to cater for human oddities.'

Identifying and satisfying the motivational needs of your salesmen is a continuous and central part of your management job. The impact you can make is considerable but it is far from simple. Nor is it like a tap you can switch on and off as the whim takes you. You cannot say, 'Thursday is my day for motivating people; today is Monday when I check last week's sales figures.'

The now famous Hawthorne Studies conducted by Elton Mayo in 1924 led to the first application of scientific study of people at work. The most revealing fact learned then remains true today: there is a handsome dividend to be earned in terms of productivity and commitment from workers by a manager who takes the trouble to consider human beings, their needs and the social and environmental factors that affect them. Do not overestimate the power of money. Never underestimate the power of true leadership, fairness, decisiveness, information, giving praise, constructive criticism and showing by example what you expect of others.

Note

[1] Lawrence J. Peter and Raymond Hull, *The Peter Principle*, Souvenir Press, 1969.

10 The sales manager

In his thought-provoking book *The Art of Captaincy* Mike Brearley draws a parallel between captaining a cricket team and sales management:

'The qualities we are looking for in our captains, as in our sales managers, are:

- How well does the candidate know how to sell and can sell?
- How well will he or she be able to motivate others to sell?

There is no one task of sales management: each has a varying degree of immediacy and importance. A sales manager cannot be 'one of the boys'. From time to time there will be unpopular decisions to make and take. He will have to say and do things that will be unpleasant for the group and possibly more so for one or two individuals. He must be prepared to promote the competent and to sack those who are not. He should always, too, be available to the team whether to listen to their ideas or to hear their complaints and anxieties'.

10.1 Defining successful sales management

In most organisations, the sales manager and his salespeople have job descriptions. But this document, however well crafted, is not a management philosophy. In a business career spanning more than forty years, I have not come across a single company that, either before appointing to or after confirming someone in a management job, gave the job holder a clear and commonly shared definition of the job of management. And without a commonly shared approach, people are either not managed at all, badly managed, or the worst traits of the worst managers are perpetuated with the result that the best people leave and go elsewhere. My own initial experiences in business with as good a company as Shell of the job of management left me puzzled as to what the job entailed. All that I do remember is that no two managers tackled the job of managing me from any recognisable set of standards.

Let me set out what is not only a simple definition of the management job, but more important, one that can be applied to any management function in any organisation. All that is needed is to replace the word 'sales' by finance, production, research and development, marketing and the definition can be applied to any of the management jobs in these areas. The Sales Management job is:

the ability to get planned sales objectives achieved through the efforts of your sales force – not for them.

There are a number of stark implications that flow from accepting such a definition. It assumes a number of things, such as:

- When you become a manager of a sales team, you have been trained to get results through other people rather than, as a salesperson, getting them for yourself and by your own efforts.
- The sales team you manage *want* to help you to achieve your planned sales objectives. (Often a big assumption.)
- By helping you to achieve your planned sales objectives, the individual, very personal and often very private motivational needs of your sales people will be met. (Again an assumption that you know what those intensely personal needs are!)

In this book I have shown how facts can be obtained to help you in these areas rather than relying on assumptions which can so often be wrong.

For a man or woman to make the translation from selling to managing a sales force successfully, a range of skills must be acquired.

What must a sales manager know and be able to do skilfully to succeed?

The place of the sales manager, and even more so that of the first line field sales manager, is a key one because:

1 He/she is the direct link between the company management, the sales force and the customer.
2 For the sales force, he/she is the *management*.
3 His/her management knowledge, skills and competence largely determine the productive efficiency of the sales force, the quality and the quantity of the selling results produced. He/she controls the selling costs, whether sales targets are met, and above all the character and morale of the sales force.

In order to accomplish all of these things, he must be a leader because he must delegate. He must be able to achieve results through other people's efforts because he cannot do everything himself. He must know:

1 how to plan and set sales objectives for the sales force;
2 how to recruit and select sales staff;
3 how to train and develop *new* and *experienced* sales personnel on-the-job;
4 how to appraise and evaluate accurately individual sales performance;
5 how to conduct off-the-job training and development;

6 how to motivate the sales force to achieve the planned sales objectives;

7 how to control the sales activities of the sales force.

It is not the purpose of this book to examine each of these sales management tasks, but only to deal with those that most directly affect the motivation of sales personnel.

But first it is necessary to consider the factors that help sales managers to decide which of the seven tasks I have listed should receive more concentration perhaps than others. Because whilst all are important, some of them should not occupy the bulk of a sales manager's time.

Four difficulties facing the sales manager

Getting planned sales objectives achieved through the sales team presents the sales manager with certain difficulties which he must recognise and deal with if he is to be successful in motivating his team to obtain them.

Difficulties	**Management implications**
1 In most companies employing a sales force, sales personnel may be geographically spread rather than working each day from an office.	● Maintaining communication. ● Motivating each person in a mainly unsupervised job. ● Maintaining control of a team so spread.
2 Selling is a highly developed social skill; it is marching the English language to war of commerce.	● In this unnatural social relationship between seller and customer, how to keep this selling skill sharp and at peak standard?
3 Customer's frequent refusal of a seller's proposition; this is particularly common in speciality selling or where there are few, if any, differences between one seller's offering and another's.	● Such refusals lead to erosion of the salesperson's selling skills and morale.
4 Sales personnel are working in unsupervised selling situations for over 90% of their working lives.	● Sales manager's priorities when accompanying individuals should be *leadership* to combat morale problems, and *training* to improve selling technique.

The relevance and degree of intensity of these four problems will obviously vary from company sales force to company sales force. You must weigh them up for yourself. But overall they provide a clue as to where sales management talents can best be invested in the limited amount of time that is available in the four *key tasks*.

1 *Training and developing* new *sales personnel*

I am talking mainly about their on-going development of selling skills once they have taken up their jobs on their sales territories after completing initial classroom training. But even here two examples, one British, one American and both leaders in their fields of commerce, indicate a distinctive approach different from others. In 1991 the Automotive Retailing operations of Shell International took as a vision to support quality management that training is a line management responsibility providing a common thread running from line managers to sales representatives through to dealers at petrol stations and their staff. Procter & Gamble is one of the most outstanding companies in the world of fast moving consumer goods marketing. In this American multi-national there is no direct route into first line sales management from the sales force. The first stage for anyone who aspires to management is to prove that he or she can train and develop sales personnel in the field assisting the Area Sales Manager. The consequence of such an approach is that until you prove that you can train and develop others, you can never move into the management of people.

One of the most endemic problems sales personnel experience when managed by newly appointed sales managers is how often, when the latter visit them on customer visits, does he take over the selling call from the sales person. He does so in the mistaken belief that by doing so a sales opportunity which he believes is going to be lost is then saved. Rarely does he consider the motivational implications that this action has on the sales person: loss of face in front of a customer; the manager going on an ego trip at the salesperson's expense; the belief that had the manager not intervened, the sales person could have obtained the sale.

2 *Training and developing experienced sales personnel*

This is probably one of the most difficult challenges that faces a manager, particularly if the sales personnel concerned are older than him. And I know this only too well. In my first field sales management appointment at the tender age of twenty-seven, I was responsible for a sales team of twelve men whose average age was fifty-seven! Every one of those twelve men were old enough to have been my father! These experienced – but not necessarily successful – people usually represent a massive financial investment by your company. Each one is the equivalent of about £50,000 a year. Now if you had such a sum of money invested in stocks and shares, how often would you monitor the performance of such an investment? Daily, I suspect. Yet if you ask the majority of sales representatives how often in the course of a month they are accompanied by their sales or field sales manager, the answer would usually be never, or at most for one day.

3 *Appraising and evaluating individual sales performance*
For everyone working in the field selling, half-yearly or annual appraisals are inadequate to develop skills and to lance morale and motivational problems arising from one of the four difficulties which I have already mentioned that sales managers have to live with in managing a sales force. There needs to be an acceptable mechanism through which you can analyse individual selling performance whenever you spend a day or more with one of your sales people accompanying them on selling visits to customers.

4 *Motivating sales staff to achieve planned sales objectives*
Through your skilful management, training and development, much more than just through pay and perks, you can motivate new sales staff to produce sales results more speedily, motivate those with management potential to develop their skills and stimulate the older, experienced sales staff so that for them selling is a progressive sales job in itself.

In carrying out these four key tasks the sales manager will be providing the two ingredients essential for sales success: *leadership* and support for men and women faced with a lonely working life isolated from day-to-day contact with the company; and *training* to develop their skill and to combat the constant wearing-down process caused by customer contact.

Bernard Shaw once wrote something, profoundly stupid: "He who can, does; he who cannot, teaches".*

Sales managers are judged not by what they can do themselves but by what they can produce through the efforts, individual and combined, of their sales forces. This can only be done by sales managers developing their knowledge and skills in the training, development and above all, motivation of sales people.

* From 'Education' Bernard Shaw

Further reading

The available books, articles and periodicals on human behaviour and aspects of motivation would fill a small library. The following list comprises publications that deal in a practical way with the subjects of recruitment and selection, training and development of salesmen, appraisal and the theories of motivation.

Theories of motivation

Herzberg, F. (1968) *Work and the Nature of Man*, Staples Press.
Herzberg, F. (1987) 'One more time: how do you motivate employees?', *Harvard Business Review*, Sept.–Oct.
McGregor, D. (1960) *The Human Side of the Enterprise*, McGraw-Hill Book Company, Maidenhead.
Maslow, A.H. (1954) *Motivation and Personality*, Harper & Row.
Taylor, F.W. 'The Principles of Scientific Management', in F.C. Copley, *Scientific Management*, Harper & Row, pp. 36–39; 100–101.
William, Paul W.J. Jnr., Robertson, B. and Herzberg, F. (1969) 'Job Enrichment Pays Off', *Harvard Business Review* March–April.

Recruitment and selection

Lidstone, J. (1983) *How to Recruit and Select Successful Salesmen*, Gower.
Webster, E.C. (1964) *Decision Making in the Employment Interview*, Industrial Relations Centre, McGill University, Montreal.
Personnel Review (1973) *Recent Insights into Selection Interview*.

Management and leadership

Brearley, M. (1985) *The Art of Captaincy*, Hodder & Stoughton.
Drucker, P. (1970) *The Practice of Management*, Pan Books.
Wilson, M.T. (1983) *Managing a Sales Force*, Gower.
Institute of Management (1976) *British Management Report*.

Sales training

Lidstone, J. (1975 and 1986) *Training Salesmen on the Job*, Gower.
Lidstone, J. (1991) *Manual of Sales Negotiation*, Gower.
Mager, R. (1962) *Preparing Instructional Objectives*, Fearour, USA.

General reading

Langley, M. (1987) *Rewarding the Sales Force*, Institute of Personnel Management.
McMurry, R. (1961) 'The Mystique of Super Salesmanship', *Harvard Business Review*, March–April.
Lord Moran, (1966) *The Anatomy of Courage*, Constable.

Index

Responsibility 7, 9, 12, 22, 32, 75, 116: advance in 77–8, 90; need for 63
Retail trade selling 16, 19
Rewards 3, 7, 8–9, 71, 90
Routine calls 72

Safety needs 5, 7, 12
Salary 11–12, 13, 29, 32, 38: basic 30; high 84; increase of 71–2, 90, 115; plus bonus 35, 38; plus commission on sales 34–5, 38
Salary levels, establishment of 31–3
Salary policy 31–2
Salary scales 29, 30–1, 32–4, 78
Sales administration 70
Sales assistant 15–16, 19
Sales bulletin 71
Sales campaign, incentive based 40
Sales conferences 49, 70–1, 89
Sales contests 89
Sales force 76: changes in 82; changing role of 48; communication with 53; and manager 81–3; mixed 113; recognition of importance of 57; reduction in 48, 53; role of 57; specialist 66; training and motivation of 76
Sales job: categories of 16–21; contribution to company by 67; difficulties of 21; insecurity of 47, 54; pioneering 51; specialist 90
Sales letter 52
Sales manager 121–5: appointment of 75, 81; attitude to sales force 81–2; checklist for security 54; competence of 47; lack of knowledge of motivation 1; leadership of 21–2, 26–8; as psychologist 90–1; supportive visits to salesmen by 51–2; task of 2, 13–14, 50–3, 76
Sales meetings 62, 70
Sales objectives 42, 44, 50, 76, 91
Sales performance 32–3, 47: feedback about 49, 69–70; recognition of 58–9; standards of 50–1, 70, 76, 87
Sales results, visibility of 47

Sales targets 2, 24–5, 32, 35, 50, 81: optimistic 69
Sales team 52, 72
Sales territories: change of 74; multinational 113
'Salesman of the year' prizes 86, 89
Salesmen: career salesmen 90; categories of 16–21; individual make-up of 26; insecurity of 47, 54; medical 66–7; selection of 83–91, 116
Satisfiers 10–11, 12
Secrecy 116: avoidance of 53
Security 13, 64: need for Ch. 5, 86; provision of 86–7
Selection decisions 83–91, 114, 116
Selection interviewing 50
Self-actualisation, self-fulfilment 6, 9, 12, 22, 63, 77
Self-confidence 19: loss of 21
Self-control 7, 8, 10
Selling 15: in areas of high technology 113; as career 21, 56; career prospects in 114; changes in 65; as social skill 21
Separation, physical and temporal, from manager 49, 91
Service 89
Servicing calls 35
Sex 5
Sex discrimination 113
Sick pay 40
Social group 55: status in 57, 67
Social security 29, 114
Speciality products, selling of 15, 17, 20, 33, 52–3
Status 13, 19, 64, 78, 120: and cultural factors 55; definition of 55; external symbols of 57–8, 77; need for Ch. 6, 89; satisfying needs for 57–62; titles 88
Stress 48: of constant travel 113
Subsistence level 29–30
Supervision 11, 25: supportive 113
Symbols 57–8, 71, 77

Takeovers 48, 91, 112, 114
Target selling 64
Taylor, F.W. 2: scientific management 2–3, 7

131